BEST of the WORSTEDS™

Edited by Bobbie Matela

HOUSE of
WHITE
BIRCHES
PUBLISHERS
SINCE 1947

BEST of the WORSTEDS™

EDITOR Bobbie Matela
ART DIRECTOR Brad Snow
PUBLISHING SERVICES DIRECTOR Brenda Gallmeyer

SENIOR EDITOR Kathy Wesley
ASSISTANT ART DIRECTOR Nick Pierce
COPY SUPERVISOR Michelle Beck
COPY EDITORS Susanna Tobias, Mary O'Donnell
TECHNICAL EDITOR Charlotte Quiggle
TECHNICAL ARTISTS Nicole Gage, Pam Gregory

GRAPHIC ARTS SUPERVISOR Ronda Bechinski
GRAPHIC ARTISTS Erin Augsburger, Joanne Gonzalez
PRODUCTION ASSISTANTS Marj Morgan, Judy Neuenschwander

PHOTOGRAPHY SUPERVISOR Tammy Christian
PHOTOGRAPHY Don Clark, Matthew Owen
PHOTO STYLISTS Tammy Smith, Tammy Steiner

CHIEF EXECUTIVE OFFICER David J. McKee
BOOK MARKETING DIRECTOR Dwight Seward

PRINTED IN CHINA
FIRST PRINTING: 2008
LIBRARY OF CONGRESS CONTROL NUMBER: 2007937553
HARDCOVER ISBN: 978-1-59217-197-2
SOFTCOVER ISBN: 978-1-59217-198-9

1 2 3 4 5 6 7 8 9

DRGbooks.com

3

Welcome

Worsted weight yarn is undeniably the premier choice for comfort, ease and stress-free knitting!

Most of us learned to knit with worsted weight yarn, a comfortable weight of yarn to use to knit—it's not too thick and not too thin, but just right. Besides, if you are like most knitters, you don't want to take forever knitting with lightweight yarn, and you don't especially like working with bulky awkward yarn and fat needles. We've chosen the best and most exciting worsted weight designs to share with you!

One of the best things about this book is that we show two yarn choices for each design. The featured yarn has been used to complete a finished project, while the option yarn is usually shown as a close-up swatch. The aim is to give you the confidence to use yarns similar to our two choices for your own unique one-of-a-kind knits. Perhaps you have already purchased yarn that you would like to use. Or maybe you have found a yarn at a great price, and you want to use that yarn. Most of the projects in this volume have a gauge of about 4½ to 5 stitches per inch. So if the yarn you want to use also has a gauge of 4½ to 5 stitches per inch, you are in business. If you are a little fuzzy on the whole stitches-per-inch gauge story, we've included information to explain it in detail.

In the years to come, if the yarns we have shown are no longer available, our hope is that you will have the confidence to use these patterns with the latest worsted weight yarns—substituting with abandon!

With best of the worsted wishes,

Bobbie Matela

Table of Contents

MARVELOUS AFGHANS & PILLOWS

The Mystery of a Worsted Gauge

It's a matter of size!

Many knitters have been happily knitting for years giving no thought to the gauge. However, in order for your project to be the size desired, you really do need to understand and pay attention to gauge.

Gauge simply means the number of stitches per inch and the number of rows per inch using a specified yarn and needle size. In this book, all designs have a gauge of about 4 to 5 stitches per inch and 6 to 8 rows per inch. The gauge given with each pattern is the gauge used by the designer. If you knit more loosely or more tightly than the designer, even if you use the very same yarn,

the measurements of your finished work will vary. Since you do not want to end up with a garment that is either too large or too small, you need to knit to the designer's gauge. This is best done by knitting a gauge swatch. Knitting a gauge swatch is like taking a test drive or going on a first date. You'll learn a lot about your yarn. Not doing a gauge swatch is like driving with a blindfold or getting married before going on a first date. You have no idea whether the outcome will be favorable.

MAKING THE SWATCH

To knit a gauge swatch, cast on the number of stitches that

you should have in 4 inches. Let's take the example of a sweater with a gauge that reads: 18 stitches and 24 rows to 4 inches/10cm in stockinette stitch, and the materials list specifies a size 7 needle (or size required for gauge). For this example, you would cast on 18 stitches and knit 24 rows. If the gauge is given for just 1 inch, cast on four times that number of stitches, and knit four times the number of rows in 1 inch.

It is always recommended that you work up a swatch at least 4 x 4 inches using the yarn and needle size that will give you the gauge. In this case, the gauge is 4½ stitches per inch (18 stitches

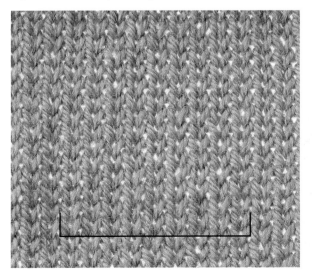

9 stitches = 2 inches

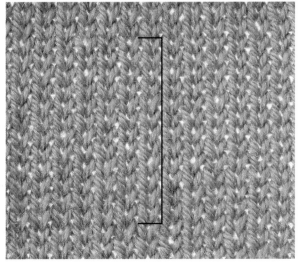

12 rows = 2 inches

5 stitches = 1 inch   **4½ stitches = 1 inch**   **4 stitches = 1 inch**

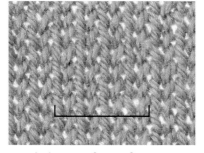

Knitting too loose for gauge   **Knitting too tight for gauge**

divided by 4 inches) and 6 rows per inch (24 rows divided by 4 inches).

Place your swatch on a flat firm surface to measure it—not the edge of a sofa or chair. An ironing board is a good place for measuring swatches. If the edges are curling, you can pin them out, being careful not to stretch it. Measure the center 2 inches of stitches horizontally to check the stitch count. Also measure vertically to check the row count.

What happens if you use the needle size specified and you don't get the gauge? At the top of this page are gauge swatch samples using the very same yarn and needle size by three different knitters.

The loosest knitter got a gauge of 4 stitches per inch

and 6 rows per inch. She will need to try again using smaller size needles.

The tightest knitter got a gauge of 5 stitches per inch and 7½ rows per inch. She will need to try again using larger size needles.

If a second try does not give you the correct gauge, try again, using larger needles if you have too many stitches, or smaller

needles if you have too few stitches. Keep in mind that this is more fun than ripping out or throwing away a project that is not wearable.

Sometimes, changing from your current needles to a different needle type will change the gauge. For example, you may knit more loosely when using metal needles than you do when using bamboo or plastic needles.

THE MYSTERY OF A WORSTED GAUGE

Swatch in pattern stitch

It is also advisable to check your gauge every couple of inches while you are knitting. This is especially important if your mood and posture affect how tightly or loosely you knit.

Sometimes the gauge is not given in stockinette stitch (St st). If that is the case simply use the stitch specified in the gauge information for your swatch. You will need to consider the multiple when casting on for your swatch.

For example, for the Tampa Vest on page 96, the gauge reads: 18 sts/27 rows = 4 inches /10cm in Chevron Lace pat **Chevron Lace** (multiple of 6 sts + 1)

Row 1 (RS): K1, *yo, ssk, k1, k2tog, yo, k1; rep from * across.
Rows 2 and 4: Purl.
Row 3: K1, *k1, yo, sk2p, yo, k2; rep from * across.
Rep Rows 1–4 for pat.
You would need to cast on 19 stitches (6 x 3 + 1), and work 3 repeats of the pattern stitch across for your swatch.

USING A DIFFERENT YARN THAN THE DESIGNER

Worsted weight yarns usually vary in gauge from 4 to 6 stitches per inch. All of the swatches shown were made with worsted weight yarn, even though the gauge varies.

When choosing a yarn, check the yarn label. American-made yarns will read something like 4½ sts/inch on #8 needles. This means that the yarn company recommends that you use size 8 needles, and when working in stockinette stitch, you will get about 4½ stitches per inch. If your yarn gauge is in centimeters, it is handy to know that 10cm equals 4 inches. Imported yarns will have this information next to crossed needles and a grid.

Diagram A

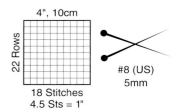

Diagram B

Yarn labels include gauge information

Since all of the projects in this book were designed with a worsted gauge, you will be able to substitute another worsted yarn for any project. But remember, not all worsted yarns are exactly the same thickness and softness. Worsted weight yarns are available in all kinds of fibers and twists. It is easiest to substitute when the yarn labels show the same gauge

(G) 4½ stitches = 1 inch

(H) 4½ stitches = 1 inch

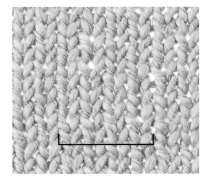

(I) 4 stitches = 1 inch

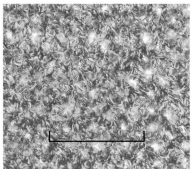

(J) 3½ stitches = 1 inch

and the yarns have a similar feel, drapability and texture. If you would like to use a yarn that is a little different in gauge (perhaps 4½ per inch instead of 5 per inch), and you think the texture will work, you simply need to change your needle size so that the gauge is the same as the gauge of your pattern.

Just remember, if your swatch is too small, use larger needles. If your swatch is too large, use smaller needles.

For each of the designs in this book we have selected an option yarn that we felt would work well for the design. If you

decide to use a different yarn, there is just a little math to do in order to know how many balls or skeins of yarn to purchase. First, look at the materials list for the featured yarn. Make note of the number of yards in each skein and the number of skeins needed for your project. Multiply these two numbers to get the **total number of yards** you need. Then, check the number of yards in the skein of yarn you want to use. If the label on the yarn you want to use specifies meters instead of yards, you will need to convert the amount in meters to the amount in yards.

Since a meter is approximately 39 inches, you can multiply the number of meters by 1.1 (the number of meters in a yard) to change it to yards. Divide that number (number of meters x 1.1) into your **total number of yards**, and you will have the number of skeins to buy.

Let's take an example of a sweater that will need 11 skeins of yarn in your size and each skein is 100 yards. Your total number of yards is 1100 (11 x 100 yards = 1100 yards).

If the yarn you want to use has 85 yards per skein, you will divide 1100 by 85 which will equal 12.9. Round up 12.9 to 13 skeins. Always round up when figuring how much yarn to buy. It is also a good idea to buy at least one extra skein—just in case. If it is left over, yarn stores will usually take yarn returns as long as you have your receipt, but there is no guarantee that they will be able to provide you with more of your yarn. Yarn companies are continually updating and discontinuing their lines of yarn.

WASHING FACTOR

If you plan to wash your project, it is a good idea to measure your swatch, wash it, then measure it again. Wash it in the same manner as you would wash the finished project. This way you can be sure it will still fit even after it has been washed.

Pampered-Baby Things

Everyone loves to knit for babies!
These are the kind soft baby knits
that make for special warm memories.
Start them now for giving at the next
baby shower.

Diagonal Eyelets Baby Set

This clever lace pattern is perfect for welcoming Baby into our world. The eyelets in the jacket also serve as the buttonholes.

Designs by Kennita Tully

SKILL LEVEL

■■■□ INTERMEDIATE

SIZES

Infant's 6 (12, 18) months Instructions are given for smallest size, with larger sizes in parentheses. When only 1 number is given, it applies to all sizes.

Option

FINISHED MEASUREMENTS
BLANKET
30 x 35 inches
JACKET
Chest: 24½ (27½, 30½) inches
Length: 11 (12, 13) inches
HAT
Circumference: Approx 15 inches

MATERIALS
- **Featured yarn:**
  Plymouth Linen Isle 50 percent cotton/30 percent rayon/20 percent linen worsted weight yarn (86 yds/50g per ball):
  For blanket: 10 balls green/purple/multicolor #9441
  For jacket and hat: 5 (5, 6) balls green/purple/multicolor #9441
- **Option yarn:**
  Plymouth Encore Worsted 75 percent acrylic/25 percent wool worsted weight yarn (200 yds/100g per ball):
  For blanket: 5 balls pink #449
  For jacket and hat: 3 balls pink #449

4 MEDIUM

- Size 6 (4mm) straight and 36-inch circular needles or size needed to obtain gauge
- Tapestry needle
- Stitch markers
- 4 (¾-inch) buttons

GAUGE
19 sts and 28 rows = 4 inches/ 10cm over Diagonal Eyelets Pat
  To save time, take time to check gauge.

PATTERN STITCH
DIAGONAL EYELETS
Version A (multiple of 10 sts + 7)
Row 1 (RS): K1, *yo, ssk, k3, p5; rep from *, end yo, ssk, k4.
Rows 2, 4, 6 and 8: K1, *p5, k5; rep from *, end p5, k1.
Row 3: K1, *k1, yo, ssk, k2, p5; rep from *, end k1, yo, ssk, k3.
Row 5: K1, *k2, yo, ssk, k1, p5; rep from *, end k2, yo, ssk, k2.
Row 7: K1, *k3, yo, ssk, p5; rep from *, end k3, yo, ssk, k1.
Row 9: K1, *p5, k3, k2tog, yo; rep from *, end k3, k2tog, yo, k1.
Rows 10, 12, 14, 16: K1, *k5, p5; rep from *, end k6.

Row 11: K1, *p5, k2, k2tog, yo, k1; rep from *, end k2, k2tog, yo, k2.
Row 13: K1, *p5, k1, k2tog, yo, k2; rep from *, end k1, k2tog, yo, k3.
Row 15: K1, *p5, k2tog, yo, k3; rep from *, end k2tog, yo, k4.
Rep Rows 1–16 for pat.

Version B (multiple of 10 sts + 2)
Row 1 (RS): K1, *yo, ssk, k3, p5; rep from *, end k1.
Rows 2, 4, 6 and 8: K1, *p5, k5; rep from *, end k1.
Row 3: K1, *k1, yo, ssk, k2, p5; rep from *, end k1.
Row 5: K1, *k2, yo, ssk, k1, p5; rep from *, end k1.
Row 7: K1, *k3, yo, ssk, p5; rep from *, end k1.
Row 9: K1, *p5, k3, k2tog, yo; rep from *, end k1.
Rows 10, 12, 14, 16: K1, *k5, p5; rep from *, end k1.
Row 11: K1, *p5, k2, k2tog, yo, k1; rep from *, end k1.
Row 13: K1, *p5, k1, k2tog, yo, k2; rep from *, end k1.
Row 15: K1, *p5, k2tog, yo, k3; rep from *, end k1.
Rep Rows 1–16 for pat.

BLANKET

PATTERN NOTE
The blanket is worked back and forth in rows; a circular needle is used to accommodate the large number of sts.

INSTRUCTIONS
With circular needle and using long-tail method, cast on 137 sts.
   Knit 3 rows.
   Following Version A, work 15 reps of Diagonal Eyelets, then work Rows 1–8 once more.

Knit 4 rows.
Bind off.

FINISHING

With circular needle, pick up and knit 194 sts along side edge then work in garter st for 3 rows. Bind off. Rep for other side edge. Darn in all ends. Wash and pin to measurements.

JACKET

BACK

Using long-tail method, cast on 57 (62, 67) sts.
Set up pat (WS): Following Version A (B, A) of Diagonal Eyelet pat, work Row 2.

Continue with Rows 1–16 of pat as established for 6 (6½, 7) inches; mark edges for armhole placement.

Continue in pat until piece measures 11 (12, 13) inches, ending with Row 8 or 16.

Bind off all sts.

FRONTS
MAKE 2
Cast on 32 (37, 42) sts.
Set up pat: Following Version B (A, B) of Diagonal Eyelet pat, work Row 2.

Continue with Rows 1–16 of pat as established until piece measures same as back, marking armhole placement as for back.

Bind off all sts.

SLEEVES
Using long-tail method, cast on 27 sts.
Set up pat: Following Version A, work Row 2.

Work Rows 1–8, then change to St st for rest of sleeve.

At the same time, inc 1 st on 2nd RS row, then [every 4 (4, 2) rows] 5 (11, 3) times, then [every 6 (0, 4) rows] 4 (0, 11) times. (47, 51, 57 sts)

Work until sleeve measures approx 8 (8½, 9) inches.

Bind off all sts.

FINISHING
Wash and block pieces to measurements.

Mark shoulders by placing markers 2½ (2¾, 3) inches to left and right of center back. Sew shoulder seams between armhole edges and markers, matching pattern.

Sew in sleeves between armhole markers.

Sew sleeve and side seams.

Fold back and tack collar down.

Sew on buttons, using the eyelets as buttonholes.

HAT

Cast on 72 sts.
Set up pat: Following Version B, work Row 2.

Work Rows 1–8 in pat as established.

Work even in St st until piece measures 3½ inches from beg.

SHAPE CROWN
Set-up row (RS): K1, *k8, k2tog, place marker; rep from *, end k1. (65 sts)
Next row: Purl.
Dec row (RS): *Knit to 2 sts before marker, k2tog; rep from * to last st, k1. (58 sts)
Rep dec row [every other row] 7 times. (9 sts)

Cut yarn, leaving a 12-inch tail.

Using tapestry needle, thread tail through rem sts, and pull tight.

Using tail, sew seam.

Weave in all ends. ∎

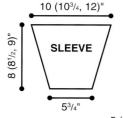

10 (10¾, 12)"

SLEEVE

8 (8½, 9)"

5¾"

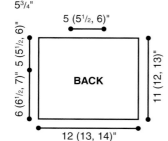

FRONT

6¾ (7¾, 8¾)"

11 (12, 13)"

5 (5½, 6)"

BACK

6 (6½, 7)" 5 (5½, 6)"

11 (12, 13)"

12 (13, 14)"

Garter Stripes Ensemble

Playful eye-catching stripes ensure that Baby will enjoy attention. Leg warmers add a fashionable, yet practical touch.

Designs by Scarlet Taylor

SKILL LEVEL
 EASY

SIZES
Cardigan: Infant's 6 (12, 18) months
Hat: Infant's 6 (12–18) months
Leg Warmers: Infant's 6–12 (18) months
For each project, instructions are given for smallest size with larger size(s) in parentheses. When only 1 number is given, it applies to both (all) sizes.

FINISHED MEASUREMENTS
CARDIGAN
Chest: 22 (24, 26) inches
Length: 9½ (11, 12) inches

BLANKET
30 x 33 inches
HAT
Circumference: 15½ (16½) inches
Depth: 5½ (6) inches
LEG WARMER
Circumference at ankle:
6½ (7) inches
Circumference at knee:
8½ (9) inches
Length: 7½ (8½) inches

MATERIALS
- **Featured yarn:**
  Plymouth Encore Worsted 75 percent acrylic/25 percent wool worsted weight yarn (200 yds/100g per ball):
  For cardigan: 1 ball each white #146 (A), lilac #1308 (B), light green #450 (C), pink #449 (D) and peach #448 (E)
  For blanket: 2 balls white #146 (A), 1 ball each lilac #1308 (B), light green #450 (C), pink #449 (D) and peach #448 (E)
  For hat and legwarmers:
  1 ball each white #146 (A), lilac #1308 (B), light green #450 (C), pink #449 (D) and peach #448 (E)

- **Option yarn:** Plymouth Fantasy Naturale 100 percent mercerized cotton worsted weight yarn (140 yds/100g per skein):
  For cardigan: 2 skeins denim #9003 (A), 3 skeins light green #5425 (B) and 2 skeins light blue #2576 (C)
  For blanket: 3 skeins each denim #9003 (A), light green #5425 (B) and light blue #2576 (C)
  For hat and leg warmers:
  1 skein each denim #9003 (A), light green #5425 (B) and light blue #2576 (C)
- Size 6 (4.25mm) straight needles
- Size 8 (5mm) straight and 29-inch circular needles or size needed to obtain gauge
- Stitch holders
- Stitch markers
- Tapestry needle
- 4 (6, 6) ¾-inch buttons

GAUGE
16 sts and 32 rows = 4 inches/10cm in pat st with larger needles
To save time, take time to check gauge.

PATTERN STITCH
Note: *Projects in Featured Yarn are worked in Garter Stripes Version*

Option

A; projects in Option Yarn are worked in Garter Stripes Version B.

GARTER STRIPES
Version A
Rows 1 (RS)–4: With B, knit. Cut B.
Row 5: With A, knit.
Row 6: With A, purl. Do not cut.
Rows 7–10: With C, knit. Cut C.
Rows 11 and 12: Rep Rows 5 and 6.
Rows 13–16: With D, knit. Cut D.
Rows 17 and 18: Rep Rows 5 and 6.

Rows 19–22: With E, knit. Cut E.
Rows 23 and 24: Rep Rows 5 and 6.
Rep Rows 1–24 for pat.

Version B
Rows 1 (RS)–4: With B, knit. Cut B.
Row 5: With A, knit.
Row 6: With A, purl. Do not cut.
Rows 7–10: With C, knit. Cut C.
Rows 11 and 12: Rep Rows 5 and 6.
Rep Rows 1–12 for pat.

PATTERN NOTES
Cardigan body is worked in 1 piece to the armholes, then divided to complete fronts and back separately.

Carry A loosely up side; cut other colors and weave in loose ends.

CARDIGAN IN FEATURED YARN

BODY
BOTTOM EDGE
With smaller straight needles and B, cast on 88 (96, 104) sts.

Work in garter st for approx ½ inch, ending with a WS row.
Next row (RS): Change to larger straight needles and, beg with row 1, work even in Garter Stripes (Version A) until piece measures 5 (6¼, 6¾) inches from beg, ending with a WS row.

DIVIDE FOR FRONTS & BACK
Next row (RS): Work 22 (24, 26) sts and place on holder for right front; work next 44 (48, 52) sts for back; place rem 22 (24, 26) sts on holder for left front.

BACK
Next row (WS): Working on back sts only, continue in pat as established, and work 1 row.

SHAPE ARMHOLES
Bind off 3 (4, 5) sts at beg of next 2 rows. (38, 40, 42 sts)

Work even until piece measures 9¼ (10¾, 11¾) inches from beg, ending with a WS row.

SHAPE BACK NECK
Work 12 (13, 13) sts, join a 2nd ball of yarn and bind off center 14 (14, 16) sts for back neck, work to end.

Working both sides at once with separate balls of yarn, dec 1 st at each neck edge once. Bind off rem 11 (12, 12) sts each side for shoulders.

RIGHT FRONT
Sl sts for right front to needle with WS facing and attach yarn.

SHAPE ARMHOLE
Next row (WS): Bind off 3 (4, 5) sts, work in pat to end of row. (19, 20, 21 sts)

Work even until piece measures 7½ (9, 10) inches from beg, ending with a WS row.

SHAPE FRONT NECK
Next row (RS): Bind off 3 sts, work in pat to end of row. (16, 17, 18 sts)

18 MONTHS SIZE ONLY
Bind off 2 sts at beg of next RS row.

ALL SIZES
Dec 1 st at neck edge every RS row 5 (5, 4) times. (11, 12, 12 sts)

Work even until piece measures same as back to shoulders.
Bind off.

LEFT FRONT

Sl sts for left front to needle with RS facing and attach yarn.

SHAPE ARMHOLE

Next row (RS): Bind off 3 (4, 5) sts, work in pat to end of row. (19, 20, 21 sts)

Work even until piece measures 7½ (9, 10) inches from beg, ending with a RS row.

SHAPE FRONT NECK

Next row (WS): Bind off 3 sts, work in pat to end of row. (16, 17, 18 sts)

18 MONTHS SIZE ONLY

Bind off 2 sts at beg of next WS row.

ALL SIZES

Dec 1 st at neck edge every RS row 5 (5, 4) times. (11, 12, 12 sts)

Work even until piece measures same as back to shoulders.

Bind off.

SLEEVES

With smaller needles and B, cast on 22 (26, 28) sts.

Work in garter st for approx ½ inch, ending with a WS row.

Next row (RS): Change to larger needles and, beg with Row 1, work Garter Stripes pat; *at the same time,* inc 1 st each side on this row, then [every 6th row]

5 (1, 1) time(s), then [every 8 row] 0 (3, 4) times. (34, 36, 40 sts)

Work even until piece measures 6¾ (7½, 8¾) inches from beg, ending with a WS row.

Bind off.

ASSEMBLY

Sew shoulder seams.

NECKBAND

With RS facing, using smaller needles and B, pick up and knit 49 (49, 51) sts evenly around neck edge.

Work in garter st for approx 1 inch.

Bind off loosely.

BUTTON BAND

Work on left front edge for girl/ right front edge for boy.

With RS facing, using smaller needles and B, pick up and knit 41 (48, 53) sts evenly along edge including neckband.

Work in garter st for approx 1 inch.

Bind off loosely.

Place markers for 4 (6, 6) buttons evenly spaced, with first and last buttons ½ inch from top and bottom edges of cardigan.

BUTTONHOLE BAND

Work on right front edge for girl/ left front edge for boy.

Work as for button band until band measures approx ½ inch.

Next row: Make buttonholes opposite markers by working yo, k2tog.

Work even until band measures approx 1 inch.

Bind off loosely.

FINISHING

Sew in sleeves; sew sleeve seams.

Sew on buttons. Wash and block.

BLANKET IN FEATURED YARN

PATTERN NOTE

A circular needle is used to accommodate large number of sts. Do not join; work the blanket back and forth in rows.

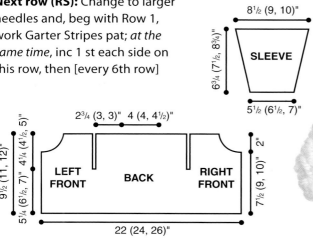

BORDER

With A, cast on 120 sts.

Work in garter st for approx 1 inch, ending with a WS row.

Set up side borders: With A, k4, place marker, join B and work Garter Stripes (Version A) to last 4 sts, place marker, join a 2nd ball of A, k4.

Continue in pats as established, maintaining first and last 4 sts in garter st in A for side borders throughout, until blanket measures approx 34 inches from beg, ending with Row 4 of Garter Stripes pat.

Next row (RS): With A only, work in garter st for approx 1 inch, ending with a WS row. Bind off loosely knitwise.

FINISHING

Neatly weave in yarn ends.

BLANKET IN OPTION YARN

Work as for Blanket in Featured Yarn but work Garter Stripes (Version B).

HAT IN FEATURED YARN

ROLLED EDGE

With B, cast on 80 (84) sts.

Work in St st for approx 1¼ inches, ending with a WS row.

BEG ST PAT & DEC FOR HAT

Next row: Beg Garter Stripes (Version A) and dec across as follows: k2 (4), k2tog, [k3, k2tog] 15 times, k1 (3). (64, 68 sts)

Work even for approx 4¼ (4¾) inches, ending with a WS row.

Cut yarns and continue in B only.

SHAPE CROWN

Dec row 1 (RS): K6, k2tog, [k3, k2tog] 10 (11) times, k6 (5). (53, 56 sts)

Next row and all WS rows: Knit.

Dec row 2: K6 (5), k2tog, [k2, k2tog] 10 (11) times, k5. (42, 44 sts)

Dec row 3: K5, k2tog, [k1, k2tog] 10 (11) times, k5 (4). (31, 32 sts)

Dec row 4: K1 (2), k2tog, [k1, k2tog] 9 times, k1. (21, 22 sts)

Dec row 5: K1, [k2tog] 9 (10) times, k2 (1). (12 sts)

I-CORD TAILS

Knit 4 I-cord tails using a different color for each tail as follows:

Sl last 9 sts to holder.

Join desired color and *k3; do not turn, sl sts back to LH needle; rep from * until cord is 2½ inches or desired length.

Bind off.

Using different colors, make 3 more 3-st I-cord tails using rem 9 sts.

FINISHING

With WS facing, sew seam of rolled edge.

With RS facing, sew rest of seam to top, matching pat.

Weave in yarn ends.

HAT IN OPTION YARN

Work as for Hat in Featured Yarn, but use A for Rolled Edge, work Garter Stripes (Version B), and use C for Crown. Make I-cord tails in colors as desired.

LEG WARMERS

With smaller straight needles and B, cast on 26 (28) sts.

Work in k1, p1 rib until piece measures approx ½ inch, ending with a WS row.

Change to larger straight needles and Garter Stripes Version A.

SHAPE LEG

Inc 1 st each side [every 10th row] 2 (0) times, then [every 12th row] 2 (2) times, then [every 14th row] 0 (2) times. (34, 36 sts)

Work even until piece measures approx 7 (8) inches from beg, ending with a WS row.

Change to smaller needles and B, then work in k1, p1 rib for approx ½ inch.

Bind off loosely in rib.

FINISHING

Sew leg seam matching pat.

Weave in loose ends. ∎

Baby Basket Beanie & Blankie

When you need a baby gift in a hurry, try this simple basket-weave stitch set. Choose either a solid or multicolored yarn for impressive results.

Designs by Nazanin Fard

SKILL LEVEL
■■□□ EASY

SIZE
Newborn

FINISHED MEASUREMENT
BLANKET
30 x 30 inches
HAT
Circumference: 9¾ inches

MATERIALS
- **Featured yarn:** Universal Yarn Inc. Classic Worsted 80 percent acrylic/ 20 percent wool worsted weight yarn (197 yds/100g per ball):
  For blanket and hat: 5 balls cream #607
- **Option yarn:** Red Heart Super Saver 100 percent acrylic worsted weight yarn (244 yds/141g per skein):
  For blanket and hat: 4 skeins Monet print #310
- Size 7 (4.5 mm) 24-inch (or longer) circular needle (for blanket) or size needed to obtain gauge
- Size 7 (4.5 mm) set of 4 double-pointed needles (for hat) or size needed to obtain gauge
- Stitch markers
- Tapestry needle

GAUGE
22 sts and 32 rows = 4 inches/10cm in pat
  To save time, take time to check gauge.

Option

PATTERN NOTE

Always sl sts purlwise, holding yarn to WS.

PATTERN STITCHES

A. Basket Weave (multiple of 6 sts + 8)
Row 1 (RS): Knit.
Row 2: K4, purl to last 4 sts, k4.
Rows 3 and 5: K4, *sl 2, k4; rep from * to last 4 sts, k4.
Rows 4 and 6: K4, *k4, sl 2; rep from * to end.
Row 7: Knit.
Row 8: Rep Row 2.
Rows 9 and 11: K4, *k3, sl 2, k1; rep from * to last 4 sts, k4.
Rows 10 and 12: K4, *k1, sl 2, k3; rep from * to last 4 sts, k4.
Rep Rows 1–12 for pat.

B. Basket Weave (in the round)
(multiple of 6 sts)
Rnds 1 and 2: Knit.
Rnds 3 and 5: *Sl 2, k4; rep from * around.
Rnds 4 and 6: *Sl 2, p4; rep from * around.
Rnds 7 and 8: Knit.
Rnds 9 and 11: *K3, sl 2, k1; rep from * around.
Rnds 10 and 12: *P3, sl 2, p1; rep from * around.
Rep Rnds 1–12 for pat.

BLANKET

PATTERN NOTES

Pat is worked back and forth; a circular needle is used to accommodate the large number of sts.
Sl sts purlwise with yarn to WS.

INSTRUCTIONS

With either Featured or Option yarn, cast on 158 sts.

Knit 6 rows.
Work even in Basket Weave pat until piece measures 29 inches.
Work even until piece measures 29 inches.
Knit 6 rows.
Bind off all sts loosely.
Block blanket to size.

HAT

With either Featured or Option yarn, cast on 54 sts.
Distribute evenly on 3 dpns, place marker for beg of rnd and join, making sure not to twist sts.
Work 10 rnds of k1, p1 rib.
Work 3 reps of 12-rnd Basket Weave (in the round) pat, then work Rnds 1 and 2 again.

CROWN

Rnd 1: *K4, k2tog; rep from * around. (45 sts)
Rnd 2: Knit.
Rnd 3: *K3, k2tog; rep from * around. (36 sts)
Rnds 4–5: Knit.
Rnd 6: K2tog around. (18 sts)
Rnd 7: Knit.

Rnd 8: Rep Rnd 6. (9 sts)
Rnd 9: *K1, k2tog; rep from * around. (6 sts)
Rnd 10: Rep Rnd 6. (3 sts)

I-CORD

Sl all 3 sts to 1 needle. *K3, do not turn, sl sts back to LH needle; rep from * for 10 rows.
Bind off.
Cut yarn, leaving a 6-inch tail.

FINISHING

Weave in all ends.
With a tapestry needle, sew the end of I-cord to the top of hat. ■

My Little Monkey Romper & Blankie

Baby will enjoy delicious mashed bananas in this hand-knitted style. The matching tuck-stitch blanket offers cozy comfort.

Designs by Cindy Polfer

SKILL LEVEL
Romper: ■■■□ EXPERIENCED
Blanket: ■■□□ INTERMEDIATE

SIZES
Infant's 6 (12, 18, 24) months
Instructions are given for smallest size, with larger sizes in parentheses. When only 1 number is given, it applies to all sizes.

FINISHED MEASUREMENTS
ROMPER
Chest: 22 (23, 24, 25) inches
Total Back Length: 15¼ (16¼, 17¼, 18¼) inches
BLANKET
33½ x 38½ inches

MATERIALS
- **Featured yarn:** Brown Sheep Cotton Fleece 80 percent cotton/20 percent wool worsted weight yarn (215 yds/100g per skein):
  For romper: 2 skeins teddy bear #CW820 (A), 1 skein each truffle #CW825 (B) and putty #CW105 (C), 10 yds buttercream #CW725 (D) and 3 yds cavern #CW005 (E)*
  For blanket: 2 skeins each teddy bear #CW820 (A), truffle #CW825 (B), putty #CW105 (C) and 1 skein buttercream #CW725 (D)
- **Option yarn:** Red Heart Super Saver 100 percent acrylic worsted weight yarn (7 oz/364 yds/198g per skein and Red

Heart Classic 3.5 oz/190 yds/99g per skein):
  For romper: 1 [7-oz] skein light raspberry #774 (A), 1 [3.5-oz] skein each mid brown #339 (B) and tan #334 (C), 10 yds yellow #230 (D) and 3 yds black #12 (E)
  For blanket: 2 [7-oz] skeins light raspberry #774 (A), 2 [3.5-oz] skeins each mid brown #339 (B) and tan #334 (C)
- Size 3 (3.25mm) straight needles
- Size 7 (4.5mm) straight needles or size needed to obtain gauge
- Size 6 (4mm) 24-inch (or longer) circular needle or size needed to obtain gauge
- Size I/9 (5.5mm) crochet hook
- 6 stitch holders
- 10 bobbins (optional)
- 2 stitch markers
- Tapestry needle
- 4½-inch piece of snap tape (3 snaps)
- Sewing needle and thread in color of snap tape
- Small amount of scrap yarn

If also making the blanket, there will be enough C or D left over to use for the romper.

Option

4 MEDIUM

GAUGE
Romper: 19 sts and 25 rows = 4 inches/10cm in St st using larger needles

Blanket: 18 sts and 36 rows = 4 inches/10cm

To save time, take time to check gauge.

SPECIAL ABBREVIATION
W&T (Wrap and Turn): With yarn on WS, sl next st purlwise, bring yarn to RS between needles, sl same st back to LH needle, bring yarn to WS between needles, turn work.

SPECIAL TECHNIQUES
Hiding short-row wraps: On RS, knit to st just before wrapped st, insert the needle under wrap and knitwise into st and knit st and wrap tog; on WS, purl to st just before wrapped st, insert the right needle from behind into back lp of wrap and place it on left needle then purl wrap and st tog.

3-Needle Bind Off: With RS tog and needles parallel, using a 3rd needle, knit tog a st from the front needle with 1 from the back. *Knit tog a st from the front and back needles, and sl the first st over the 2nd to bind off. Rep from * across, then fasten off last st.

PATTERN STITCHES
A. Striped Rib (odd number of sts)

Row 1 (WS): With B, k1, *p1, k1; rep from * across.

Row 2 (RS): With B, p1, *k1, p1; rep from * across.

Row 3: With C, purl.

Row 4: With C, p1, *k1, p1; rep from * across.

Row 5: With B, purl.

Row 6: With B, p1, *k1, p1; rep from * across.

Row 7: With B, k1, *p1, k1; rep from * across.

B. Tuck Pat (multiple of 4 sts + 3)

Row 1 (RS): With new color, k3, *knit into st 4 rows below st on needle, dropping the st on needle, k3; rep from * across row.

Row 2: Purl.

Row 3: Knit.

Row 4: Purl.

Row 5: With new color, k1, *knit into st 4 rows below needle, dropping st from needle, k3; rep from * across row, ending with knit into st below st on needle, dropping st from needle, k1.

Row 6: Purl.

Row 7: Knit.

Row 8: Purl.

Rep Rows 1–8 for pat, changing colors every 4 rows.

PATTERN NOTES
When working monkey motif, use intarsia technique, using separate lengths of yarn (on bobbins if desired) for each colored section; bring new color up from under old color to lock them. The black (mouth, eyes and tips of bananas) may be duplicate-stitched afterwards instead of knitting them into garment.

The sts of the folded collar are not bound off, but left open and tacked to base of neckline to ensure a stretchy neck that will sl easily over a child's head.

ROMPER

BACK
CROTCH FACING
With larger straight needles and A, cast on 11 sts.

Beg with a RS row, work 6 rows in St st.

Purl 1 row for turning ridge.

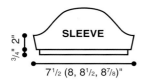

SLEEVE

2"
³/₄"

7¹/₂ (8, 8¹/₂, 8⁷/₈)"

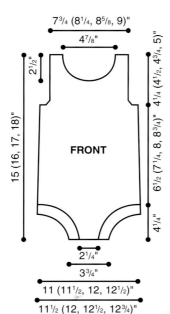

7³/₄ (8¹/₄, 8⁵/₈, 9)"
4⁷/₈"
2¹/₂"
4¹/₄ (4¹/₂, 4³/₄, 5)"
15 (16, 17, 18)"
6¹/₂ (7¹/₄, 8, 8³/₄)"
4¹/₄"
FRONT
2¹/₄"
3³/₄"
11 (11¹/₂, 12, 12¹/₂)"
11¹/₂ (12, 12¹/₂, 12³/₄)"

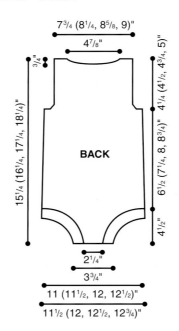

7³/₄ (8¹/₄, 8⁵/₈, 9)"
4⁷/₈"
³/₄"
4¹/₄ (4¹/₂, 4³/₄, 5)"
15¹/₄ (16¹/₄, 17¹/₄, 18¹/₄)"
6¹/₂ (7¹/₄, 8, 8³/₄)"
4¹/₂"
BACK
2¹/₄"
3³/₄"
11 (11¹/₂, 12, 12¹/₂)"
11¹/₂ (12, 12¹/₂, 12³/₄)"

MAIN BODY

Beg with a WS row, continue in St st for 9 rows.

SHAPE LEG OPENINGS

Inc 1 st each side [every other row] 5 times, then [every row] 5 times. (31 sts)

Cast on 4 sts at beg of next 6 (4, 2, 0) rows, then 5 sts at beg of following 0 (2, 4, 6) rows. (55, 57, 59, 61 sts)

Work even in St st for 2½ (2¾, 3¼, 3¾) inches, ending with a WS row.

Next row: Dec 1 st each side. (53, 55, 57, 59 sts)

Work even until piece measures 6½ (7¼, 8, 8¾) inches from top of leg opening, ending with a WS row.

SHAPE ARMHOLE

Bind off 4 sts at beg of next 2 rows. (45, 47, 49, 51 sts)

Dec 1 st each side [every other row] 4 times. (37, 39, 41, 43 sts)

Work even until armhole measures 3½ (3¾, 4, 4¼) inches, ending with a WS row.

SHAPE BACK NECK

K9 (10, 11, 12); attach a 2nd ball of yarn and k19 sts, then place these 19 sts on holder for back of neck; knit to end of row.

Working each side with separate ball of yarn, dec 1 st at each neck edge [every other row] 2 times. (7, 8, 9, 10 sts each shoulder)

Work 1 row even.

Place shoulder sts onto st holders.

FRONT

Work same as back through shaping of leg opening, except

work 7 rows (instead of 9) between turning ridge and leg shaping. (55, 57, 59, 61 sts)

Work 2 (8, 14, 18) rows even in St st.

BEG MONKEY MOTIF

Next row (RS): K10 (11, 12, 13), place marker, work across the 35 sts of first row of chart changing colors as charted, place marker, k10 (11, 12, 13).

Continue working motif between markers, and *at the same time,* when piece measures

2½ (2¾, 31/4, 3¾) inches from top of leg opening, dec 1 st each side of next row. (53, 55, 57, 59 sts)

Work even until piece measures 6½ (7¼, 8, 8¾) inches from top of leg opening, ending with a WS row.

SHAPE ARMHOLE

Bind off 4 sts at beg of next 2 rows.

Dec 1 st each side [every other row] 4 times. (37, 39, 41, 43 sts)

Work even until armhole measures 1¾ (2, 2¼, 2½) inches.

SHAPE FRONT NECKLINE

Work 11 (12, 13, 14) sts; place center 15 sts onto st holder for front neck; attach a separate ball of yarn, and work rem 11 (12, 13, 14) sts.

Working each side with separate balls of yarn, dec 1 st at each neck edge [every other row] 4 times. (7, 8, 9, 10 sts each shoulder)

Work even until armhole measures 4¼ (4½, 4¾, 5) inches, ending with a WS row. Place sts on st holders.

SLEEVES

With smaller straight needles and B, cast on 35 (37, 37, 39) sts.

Work 7 rows of Striped Rib.

Next row (RS): With A and larger straight needles, knit and inc 1 (1, 3, 3) st(s) evenly across row. (36, 38, 40, 42 sts)

Continue in St st and inc 1 st each side [every other row] 5 times. (46, 48, 50, 52 sts)

Work even until sleeve measures 2¾ inches from beg, ending with a WS row.

SHAPE CAP

Bind off 4 sts at the beg of the next 2 rows.

Dec 1 st each side [every other row] twice, ending with a WS row. (34, 36, 38, 40 sts)

SHORT ROW SHAPING

Next row: K31 (32, 34, 36) sts, W&T; p28 (28, 30, 32), W&T; k24 (24, 26, 28), W&T; p20 (20, 22, 24), W&T; k16 (16, 18, 19), W&T; p12 (12, 14, 14), W&T; knit to end of row hiding wraps as you come to them.

Next row (WS): Purl across row hiding wraps as you come to them.

Bind off all sts.

ASSEMBLY

Join right shoulders using 3-needle bind off.

COLLAR

With RS facing, using smaller straight needles and B and beg at shoulder of left-front neck edge, pick up and knit 14 sts from left front, knit center 15 sts, pick up and knit 14 sts from right front, pick up and knit 5 sts from right back, knit 19 sts from center back, and pick up and knit 4 sts from left back. (71 sts)

Work Rows 1–7 of Striped Rib Pat, then rep [Rows 6 and 7] 3 times, then work Row 6 once more. (14 rows total in band)

Do not bind off.

With WS facing, using scrap yarn and beg with a knit row, work 5 rows of St st. Cut scrap yarn and remove sts from needle.

Note: *The scrap yarn acts as a stitch holder and will be unraveled after last row of collar sts are tacked to neckline.*

Join left shoulders using 3-needle bind off.

Sew collar seam.

Fold collar in half to inside and tack last row of ribbing sts to base of collar, folding back scrap yarn as you st. Unravel scrap yarn.

Set in sleeves. Sew side and sleeve seams.

LEG OPENING BANDS

With RS facing, using smaller straight needles and B, pick up and knit 61 (63, 65, 69) sts along edge of leg opening.

Work 7 rows of Striped Rib.

With B, bind off in rib.

FINISHING

Weave in ends. Duplicate-st eyes, mouth, and tips of bananas if

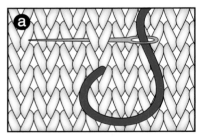

Duplicate Stitch

From Underneath piece, bring yarn up in the center of the stitch below the stitch to be duplicated. Place needle from right to left behind both sides of the stitch above the one being duplicated, and pull yarn through (a). Complete the stitch by returning the needle to where you began (b).

needed (see Fig. 1). Tack down crotch facing. Center and sew snap tape to crotch with bottom of front overlapping back, tucking under excess tape at each edge.

Block.

BLANKET IN FEATURED YARN

PATTERN NOTES

Blanket is worked back and forth; a circular needle is used to accommodate the large number of sts.

The pat st is worked in 3 colors, each having 4 rows. Carry colors not in use along edge of knitting.

When a st is dropped, the yarn strands are "tucked" into the st knitted; make sure you drop the st from the needle when you knit into the st below, or you will find you will be adding extra sts to your knitting.

INSTRUCTIONS

With B, cast on 135 sts.

Beg with a RS row, work 4 rows in St st.

Work 168 rows of Tuck Pat working 4 rows each of each color in the following sequence: C, A, B. **Note:** *The 8-row pat st will be repeated 21 times, and the 12-row color sequence will be repeated 14 times.*

Final row (RS): With B (last color knitted in sequence), rep Row 1 of pat.

With B, bind off all sts purlwise.

SHELL EDGING

With RS facing and using crochet hook, join D in upper right-hand corner of top edge and sc in corner.

Rnd 1 (top edge): Work 6 dc in 4th knit st from corner (a tucked st),

skip 3 knit sts, sc in next st, *skip 3 sts, work 6 dc in next st, skip 3 knit sts, sc in next st, rep from * across, working last sc in corner (side edge); skip 8 rows along edge (2 color changes), work 6 dc between rows of color change, skip 8 rows, sc between rows of change; rep from * to next corner, working last sc in corner; work bottom edge same as top edge and 2nd side edge same as first; join with sl st in beg corner sc. Fasten off.

Rnd 2: With RS facing, join B in first dc to left of joining, *sc in the 1st and 2nd dc of shell, work 2 sc in each of the next 2 dc, sc in each of the last 2 dc of the shell,

skip sc; rep from * around, join with sl st to first sc. Fasten off.

FINISHING

Weave in ends. Block.

BLANKET IN OPTION YARN

Work as for blanket in Featured Yarn, but with 3 colors only as follows:

Cast on with B, work 4 rows in St st, then work in color sequence C, A, B, ending with B on last row and bind off. Work Rnd 1 of shell edging with A and Rnd 2 with B. ■

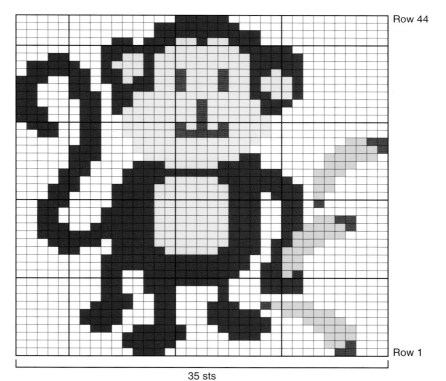

Row 44

Row 1

35 sts

My Little Monkey Chart

COLOR KEY	
☐	Teddy bear (A)
■	Truffle (B)
☐	Putty (C)
▨	Buttercream (D)
▦	Cavern (E)

OPTION COLOR KEY	
☐	Light raspberry (A)
■	Mid brown (B)
☐	Tan (C)
▨	Yellow (D)
▦	Black (E)

Precious Bundle Set

Keep Baby comfy cozy from head to toe! This wonderful gift set includes blanket, hat, sweater and booties.

Designs by Kennita Tully

SKILL LEVEL

■■■□ INTERMEDIATE

SIZES

Infant's 6 (12, 18) months Instructions are given for smallest size, with larger sizes in parentheses. When only 1 number is given, it applies to all sizes.

FINISHED MEASUREMENTS

BLANKET

Approx 35 x 33 inches

Option

JACKET

Chest: 24½ (26, 27½) inches
Length: 11 (12, 13) inches

HAT

Circumference: Approx 14 inches (relaxed)

MATERIALS

- **Featured yarn:** S. R. Kertzer Super 10 Cotton 100 percent mercerized cotton worsted weight yarn (249 yds/125g per skein):
  For blanket: 4 skeins surf #3777
  For jacket, hat and booties: 2 (2, 3) skeins surf #3777
- **Option yarn:** Red Heart Fiesta 73 percent acrylic/27 percent nylon worsted weight yarn (316 yds/170g per skein):
  For blanket: 4 skeins baby white #6301
  For jacket, hat and booties: 2 (2, 3) skeins baby white #6301
- Size 6 (4mm) straight and set of 5 double-pointed needles (for booties) or size needed to obtain gauge
- Size 7 (4.5mm) 29-inch circular needle

- Size 8 (5mm) 29-inch circular needle or size needed to obtain gauge
- Stitch holders
- Tapestry needle

GAUGE

20 sts and 33 rows = 4 inches/10cm in Jewel Cross Rib pat with larger needle
   19 sts and 26 rows = 4 inches/10cm in rib pat (Rows 1 and 2 of pat) with larger needle
   20 sts and 24 rows = 4 inches/10cm in St st with smaller needle
   To save time, take time to check gauge.

PATTERN NOTE

Always sl sts purlwise, holding yarn to WS.

SPECIAL ABBREVIATIONS

(N1, N2, N3, N4): Needle 1, Needle 2, Needle 3, Needle 4
Inc (Increase 1): Knit in front and back of st.

PATTERN STITCH

Jewel Cross Rib (multiple of 7 sts + 5)
Rows 1, 3 and 5 (WS): P5, *k2, p5; rep from * across.

Rows 2, 4 and 6 (RS): Knit.
Rows 7 and 9: K4, *sl 1, k2, sl 1, k3; rep from *, end last rep k4.
Row 8: K4, *sl 1, k2, sl 1, k3; rep from *, end last rep k4.
Row 10: K4, *drop first sl st to front of work, transfer next 2 sts to RH needle, pick up first dropped sl st with RH needle, drop 2nd sl st to front of work, transfer 3 sts back to LH needle, knit 2nd dropped sl st, knit next 3 sts on LH needle, k3; rep from *, end last rep k4.
Rep Rows 1–10 for pat.

BLANKET

PATTERN NOTE
Circular needle used to accommodate sts; do not join. Work back and forth in rows.

INSTRUCTIONS
With larger circular needles, cast on 173 sts.
   Work in Jewel Cross Rib until piece measures approximately 32 inches, ending with Row 6.
   Bind off all sts in pat.

FINISHING
With smaller circular needles, pick up and knit 172 sts along cast-on edge.
   Work in garter st for 4 rows.
   Bind off all sts.
   Rep for bound-off edge.
   For sides, pick up and knit 178 sts; work in garter st for 4 rows.
   Bind off all sts.

JACKET

PATTERN NOTE
Jacket body is knit in 1 piece to armhole then divided for yoke.

INSTRUCTIONS
BODY
With larger circular needle, cast on 117 (124, 131) sts.

Work Rows 1 and 2 of Jewel Cross Rib pat until piece measures approximately 1½ inches, ending with Row 2.

Work Rows 7–10.

Work Rows 1–10.

Rep Rows 1 and 2 only until piece measures approximately 6 (6½, 7) inches, ending with a WS row.

RIGHT FRONT YOKE

Work in pat across 29 (31, 33) sts. Place rem sts on holder.

Work additional ½ (1, 1½) inch(es) in pat.

SHAPE NECK

At neck edge, dec 1 st [every other row] 12 (13, 14) times. (17, 18, 19 sts)

Work even until piece measures 11 (12, 13) inches from beg.

Bind off all sts.

BACK YOKE

With RS facing, work in pat across next 59 (62, 65) sts for back. Work even until back measures same as right front.

Bind off all sts.

LEFT FRONT YOKE

Work in pat across rem 29 (31, 33) sts.

Work additional ½ (1, 1½) inch(es) in pat.

SHAPE NECK

At neck edge, dec 1 st [every other row] 12 (13, 14) times. (17, 18, 19 sts)

Work even until piece measures same as right front.

Bind off all sts.

SLEEVES

With larger circular needles, cast on 26 sts and work Rows 3–10 of Jewel Cross Rib pat.

Work Rows 1–10 of pat.

Continue to rep Rows 1 and 2 only of pat, *at the same time*, inc 1 st each side on RS [every 4 (4, 2) rows] 9 (13, 3) times, then [every 6 (0, 4) rows] 2 (0, 12) times. (48, 52, 56 sts)

Work even in pat until sleeve measures 8 (8½, 9) inches.

Bind off all sts.

ASSEMBLY

Sew shoulders, matching pat. Sew in sleeves and sleeve underarm seams.

BUTTON BAND

With RS facing, beg at lower edge of right front and using smaller circular needle, pick up and knit 2 sts for every 3 rows along right front, 23 (25, 27) sts along neck edge, 25 (26, 27) sts across back neck, 23 (25, 27) sts along left neck and 2 sts for every 3 rows along left front.

Next row (WS): Knit.

Next row (RS): Work 4 buttonholes by working [k2tog, yo] evenly spaced in right-front band (for girl) or left-front band (for boy), beg 4 sts from bottom and ending at beg of neck shaping, complete row.

Work 2 rows of garter st.

Bind off all sts.

FINISHING

Sew on buttons. Wash and block to measurements.

HAT

BODY

With larger circular needles, cast on 74 sts. Beg Row 1 of pat with p6 and end last rep with k2, p3.

Work Rows 2–10 of Jewel Cross Rib pat working these extra edge sts in pat.

Work Rows 1–10.

Work Rows 1–6.

SHAPE TOP

Row 1: K2, *k8, k2tog; rep from *, end k2.

Row 2: Purl.

Row 3: K2, *k7, k2tog; rep from *, end k2.

Row 4: Purl.

Row 5: K2, *k6, k2tog; rep from *, end k2.

Row 6: Purl.

Continue to work in St st in same manner, dec every other row and working 1 st fewer between dec until 32 sts rem, then dec every row until 11 sts rem.

FINISHING

Cut yarn, leaving a 12-inch end for seaming; thread yarn through tapestry needle. Run end through all sts and secure.

Sew side seam.

BOOTIES

INSTRUCTIONS

With straight needles, cast on 26 (26, 33) sts, and work 3 rows of garter st.

Work 7 rows of Jewel Cross Rib pat, beg with Row 5 and ending with Row 1 of next rep.

6 MONTHS SIZE ONLY

Next row: Work across row, dividing sts onto 4 dpn and dec as follows: Ssk, knit to last 2 sts, k2tog. (24 sts)

12 MONTHS SIZE ONLY

Next row: Work across row, dividing sts onto 4 dpn and inc as follows: K1, inc, knit to last 2 sts, inc, k1. (28 sts)

18 MONTHS SIZE ONLY

Next row: Work across row, dividing sts onto 4 dpn and dec as follows: Knit to last 2 sts, k2tog. (32 sts)

ALL SIZES

Next rnd: Join and knit around.

DIVIDE FOR HEEL

Sl first 12 (14, 16) sts to 1 needle for heel, leave rem 12 (14, 16) sts on 2 needles.

Row 1: Working on heel sts only, *sl 1, k1; rep from * across, turn.

Row 2: Sl 1, purl to end, turn.

Rows 3–8 (10, 12): [Rep Rows 1 and 2] 3 (4, 5) times.

TURN HEEL

Row 1: Sl 1, k7 (8, 9), ssk, turn.

Row 2: Sl 1, p4, p2tog, turn.

Row 3: Sl 1, k4, ssk, turn.

Row 4: Sl 1, p4, p2tog, turn.

Rep Rows 3 and 4 until 6 sts rem, ending with a WS row.

Next rnd: N1: knit across these 6 sts, pick up and knit 4 (5, 6) sts along edge of heel flap for gusset; N2: knit across 6 (7, 8) sts; N3: knit across 6 (7, 8) sts; N4: pick up and knit 4 (5, 6) sts along other side of heel flap, then knit across next 3 sts from first needle. (26, 30, 34 sts)

SHAPE GUSSET

Rnd 1: N1: knit to last 3 sts, k2tog, k1; N2 and N3: knit across (instep); N4: k1, ssk, knit to end.

Rnd 2: Knit.

Rep these 2 rnds until 24 (26, 30) sts rem.

Work even in St st until foot measures 2¾ (2¾, 3¼) inches or 1 inch less than desired length.

SHAPE TOE

Rnd 1: N1: work to last 3 sts, k2tog, k1; N2: k1, ssk, knit across; N3: knit to last 3 sts, k2tog, k1; N4: k1, ssk, knit across.

Rnd 2: Knit.

Rep last 2 rnds until 8 (10, 10) sts rem. Cut yarn, leaving a 5-inch end.

FINISHING

Thread tapestry needle and draw through rem sts and fasten off. Sew cuff seam. ∎

On-the-Go Baby Set

This contemporary color-block design is equally wonderful in bright colors to stimulate baby or in soft colors to soothe.

Designs by Kathy Perry

SKILL LEVEL

 EASY

SIZES

Infant's 6 (12, 18) months
Instructions are given for smallest size, with larger sizes in parentheses. When only 1 number is given, it applies to all sizes.

FINISHED MEASUREMENTS

SWEATER

Chest: 20 (21, 22) inches
Length: 11½ (12½, 13½) inches

HAT

Circumference: 16 (17, 17) inches

BLANKET

30 x 35 inches

MATERIALS

Option

- **Featured yarn:** Caron International Simply Soft Brites 100 percent acrylic worsted weight yarn (315 yds/6 oz per skein):

  For sweater and hat: 1 skein each limelight #9607 (A), berry blue #9609 (B) and lemonade #9606 (C)

  For blanket: 1 skein each limelight #9607 (A), berry blue #9609 (B) and lemonade #9606 (C)

- **Option yarn:** Bernat Organic Cotton 100 percent organic cotton worsted weight yarn (87 yds/50g per ball):

  For hat: 1 ball each muslin #43006 (A), hemp #43010 (B) and desert bloom #43427 (C)

  For blanket: 4 balls desert bloom #43427 (C) and 8 balls prairie rose #43426 (D)

- Size 8 (5mm) straight needles and 29-inch circular needle (blanket only) or size needed to obtain gauge
- Size 10 (6mm) 16-inch circular needle (sweater collar only)
- Size H/8 (5mm) crochet hook (for blanket only)
- Stitch holders
- Tapestry needle
- Needle and thread

GAUGE

18 sts and 24 rows = 4 inches/10cm in St st

To save time, take time to check gauge.

SPECIAL TECHNIQUE

Pompoms (for hat and blanket)

Cut 2 cardboard circles to desired diameter. Cut a hole in the center of each circle, about ½ inch in diameter. Thread a tapestry needle with a length of yarn doubled. Holding both circles tog, insert needle through center hole, over the outside edge, through center again until entire circle is covered and center hole is filled (thread more length of yarn as needed).

With sharp scissors, cut yarn between the 2 circles all around the circumference.

Using two 12-inch strands of yarn, sl yarn between circles and overlap yarn ends 2 or

3 times to prevent knot from slipping, pull tightly and tie into a firm knot. Remove cardboard and fluff out pompom by rolling it between your hands. Trim even with scissors, leaving tying ends for attaching pompom to project.

PATTERN STITCH (FOR SWEATER)

K1, P1 Rib (multiple of 2 sts)

Row 1 (RS): *K1, p1; rep from * across.

Row 2: Knit the knit sts and purl the purl sts as they face you. Rep Row 2 for rib.

SWEATER

BACK/FRONT

MAKE 2 ALIKE

With straight needles and A, cast on 48 (50, 52) sts.

Work even in K1, P1 Rib until piece measures 7½ (8¼, 9) inches, ending with a WS row.

Change to B and work even for 2 (2¼, 2½) inches, ending with a WS row.

SHAPE NECK & SHOULDERS

Work 19 (20, 21) sts; sl the next 10 sts to a holder; with a 2nd ball of yarn, work rem 19 (20, 21) sts.

Working both sides at once, dec 1 at neck edge [every row] 5 times. (14, 15, 16 sts)

Work even until armhole (section in B) measures 4 (4¼, 4½) inches.

Bind off.

SLEEVES

With straight needles and C, cast on 25 (27, 29) sts.

Work K1, P1 Rib for 1½ inches.

Change to A and St st.

Inc 1 st each side [every 5 rows] 6 (5, 6) times, then [every 0 (6, 0) rows] 0 (1, 0) time(s). (37, 39, 41 sts)

Work even until sleeve measures 6½ (7½, 8) inches from beg.

Bind off all sts.

ASSEMBLY

Sew shoulder seams.

COLLAR

With RS facing, using larger circular needle and C, and beg in center of sts on front neck holder, k5 across (right) front neck holder, pick up and knit 10 sts from right-front neck edge and 10 sts from right-back neck edge, k10 from back neck holder, pick up and knit 10 sts from left-back neck edge and 10 sts from left-front neck edge, knit 4 sts from (left) front neck holder, then knit in front and back of last st on holder. (61 sts)

Work in K1, P1 Rib for 3½ inches. Bind off all sts very loosely.

Sew sleeves to upper section in B. Sew side and underarm seams. Let bottom edge roll naturally.

FINISHING

Weave in all ends and block to measurements.

HAT

With straight needles and A, cast on 73 (78, 78) sts.

HEM

Work in St st for 4 inches.

Change to B and work in St st for 3 inches, ending with a WS row.

Next row: *K3, k2tog; rep from * across, end k3. (59, 63, 63 sts)

Work even until B measures 6 (6½, 7) inches.

Bind off, leaving a 15-inch tail.

FINISHING

Using tail end, make a running st through top row of sts, gathering tightly.

Using same tail, sew back seam of B section, then use A to sew back seam of A section.

Fold bottom half of hem to WS and tack in place at color-change row.

Make 1 medium-sized (about 2½ inch diameter) pompom in each color; join the 3 pompoms tog to make 1 large pompom and sew to top.

Using 3 strands of A, braid a cord 8 inches long. Make 2 small pompoms (about 1 inch diameter), 1 each in A and C and attach to ends of braid. Tie braid around large pompom.

BLANKET IN FEATURED YARN

PATTERN NOTES

The blanket is worked back and forth; a circular needle is used to accommodate the large number of sts.

This blanket is worked with intarsia technique, using separate balls of yarn for each colored section; bring new color up from under old color to lock them.

BORDER

With smaller circular needle and C, cast on 148 sts.

Work even in St st for 2½ inches, ending with a WS row. Cut C.

SQUARES

Change to A and k74, drop A; join B and k74 sts.

Work even in St st with 74 sts in A and 74 sts in B until A/B section measures 15 inches, ending with a WS row.

Next row (RS): K74 B, k74 A.

Work even until B/A section measures 15 inches, ending with a WS row. Cut A and B.

BORDER

Change to C and work even for 2½ inches.

Bind off.

FINISHING
SIDE HEMS

Turn over 6 sts along the side edges and tack down using needle and thread.

With C, work 2 rows sc along top and bottom edges.

With C, make 10 pompoms and sew 5 each to top and bottom borders, about 1½ inch from edge.

BLANKET IN OPTION YARN

Work as for Blanket in Featured Yarn, but instead of working squares, work 30 inches with D only. ∎

Playtime Baby Set

A knitted block is fun for Baby's first attempts at "playing catch." The easy-knit blanket and sweater will put Baby on the best-dressed list.

Designs by E. J. Slayton

SKILL LEVEL

 EASY

SIZES

Infant's 6 (12, 18) months
Instructions are given for smallest size, with larger sizes in parentheses. When only 1 number is given, it applies to all sizes.

FINISHED MEASUREMENTS

BLANKET

Approx 36 x 44 inches

JACKET

Chest: 22 (25, 27¼) inches
Length: 11 (11¾, 12½) inches

CUBE

Approx 5 inches square

MATERIALS

- **Featured yarn:** Bernat Cottontots Ombre 100 percent cotton worsted weight yarn (150 yds/85g per ball):
  For blanket: 3 balls jelly belly #91322 (A)
  For cube: 1 ball jelly belly #91322 (A)
- **Featured yarn:** Bernat Cottontots Solid 100 percent cotton worsted weight yarn (171 yds/100g per ball):

  For blanket: 2 balls each blue berry #90129 (B), lime berry #90712 (C) and grape berry #90321 (D)
  For jacket: 2 balls blue berry #90129 (B)
  For cube: 1 ball lime berry #90712 (C), grape berry #90321 (D) and small amount of blue berry #90129 (B) (for seaming)
- **Option yarn:** Plymouth Galway Worsted 100 percent wool worsted weight yarn (210 yds/100g per ball):
  For blanket: 3 balls light yellow #88 (A), 2 balls each pink #135 (B), lime green #146 (C) and orange #154 (D)
  For jacket: 2 balls color of choice
  For cube: 1 ball each pink #135 (B), lime green #146 (C) and orange #154 (D) and small amount of light yellow #88 (A) (for seaming)

Option

- Size 7 (4mm) 24-inch (or longer) circular needle (for blanket) or size needed to obtain gauge
- Size 9 (5.5mm) needles (for cube in option yarn)
- Stitch markers
- Stitch holders
- 1 (⅝-inch) button (for jacket)
- Tapestry needle

GAUGE

17 sts and 24 rows = 4 inches/10cm in pat
  To save time take time to check gauge.

SPECIAL ABBREVIATIONS

K1B (Knit 1 in Row Below): K1 in st 1 row below st on LH needle, sl both sts off LH needle. (Fig. 1).

M1 (Make 1): Inc by making a backward lp over right needle.

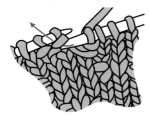

Fig. 1

SPECIAL TECHNIQUE
3-Needle Bind Off

With RS tog and needles parallel, using a 3rd needle, knit tog a st from the front needle with 1 from the back. *Knit tog a st from the front and back needles, and sl the first st over the 2nd to bind off. Rep from * across, then fasten off last st.

PATTERN STITCHES
FOR JACKET

Little Bows (multiple of 6 sts + 7)
Row 1 (WS): P2, k3, *p3, k3; rep from * to last st, end p2.
Row 2: K2, p1, k1B, p1, *k3, p1, k1B, p1; rep from * to last st, end k2.
Row 3: Purl.
Row 4: Knit.
Row 5: P5, k3, *p3, k3; rep from * to last 4 sts, end p5.
Row 6: K5, p1, k1B, p1, *k3, p1, k1B, p1; rep from * to last 4 sts, end k5.

Rows 7 and 8: Rep Rows 3 and 4.
Rep Rows 1–8 for pat.

FOR CUBE

Little Bows (multiple of 6 sts + 5)
Row 1 (WS): P1, k3, *p3, k3; rep from * to last st, end p1.
Row 2: K1, p1, k1B, p1, *k3, p1, k1B, p1; rep from * to last st, end k1.
Row 3: Purl.
Row 4: Knit.
Row 5: P4, k3, *p3, k3; rep from * to last 4 sts, end p4.
Row 6: K4, p1, k1B, p1, *k3, p1, k1B, p1; rep from * to last 4 sts, end k4.
Rows 7 and 8: Rep Rows 3 and 4.
Rep Rows 1–8 for pat.

BLANKET

PATTERN NOTE
Pat is worked back and forth; a circular needle is used to accommodate the large number of sts.

INSTRUCTIONS
With A and circular needle, cast on 155 sts.
Rows 1 (RS)–8: With A, knit.
Row 9: With B, knit.
Row 10: K3, purl to last 3 sts, k3.
Row 11: Knit.
Row 12: K3, p1, k3, *p3, k3; rep from * to last 4 sts, p1, k3.
Row 13: K4, p1, k1B, p1, *k3, p1, k1B, p1; rep from * to last 4 sts, k4.
Row 14: K3, purl to last 3 sts, k3.
Row 15: Knit.
Row 16: K3, p4, k3, *p3, k3; rep from * to last 7 sts, p4, k3.
Row 17: K7, p1, k1B, p1, *k3, p1, k1B, p1; rep from * to last 7 sts, end k7.
Rows 18 and 19: Rep Rows 14 and 15.

Rows 20–27: Rep Rows 12–19.
Row 28: K3, purl to last 3 sts, k3.
Rows 29–56: Rep Rows 1–28 using C instead of B.
Rows 57–84: Rep Rows 1–28 using D instead of B.
[Rep Rows 1–84] twice.
Rep Rows 1–28.
Rep Rows 1–8.
Bind off.

JACKET

PATTERN NOTE
When inc or dec, work any partial pat reps in St st.

BACK
BORDER
Cast on 47 (53, 59) sts.
Beg with a WS row, knit 6 rows (3 ridges of garter st); inc 1 st at each edge on last row. (49, 55, 61 sts)
Purl 1 row, knit 1 row.

BODY
Work in Little Bows pat for jacket until back measures approx 4 (4½, 5) inches from beg, ending with Row 3 or 7.

SIDE SHAPING
Beg on next row and maintaining established pat, dec 1 st at each side (k1, ssk, knit to last 3 sts, k2tog, k1) [every 8th row] 3 times. (43, 49, 55 sts)
Work even in pat until back measures approx 7 (7½, 8) inches from beg, ending with a WS row.

ARMHOLE SHAPING
Bind off 4 sts at beg of next 2 rows. (35, 41, 47 sts)
Work even in pat until armhole measures approx 4 (4¼, 4¾)

inches from underarm, ending with Row 3 or 7.

Place first 9 (12, 14) sts on holder for shoulder; place center 17 (17, 19) sts for back neck on holder, place rem sts on holder for shoulder.

RIGHT FRONT
BORDER
Cast on 23 (29, 35) sts.

Beg with WS row, knit 6 rows; inc 1 st at each edge on last row. (25, 31, 37 sts)

Purl 1 row, knit 1 row.

BODY
Work in Little Bows pat until front measures approx 4 (4½, 5) from beg, ending with Row 3 or 7.

SIDE SHAPING
Beg on next row and maintaining established pat, dec 1 st at end of row (knit to last 3 sts, k2tog, k1) [every 8th row] 3 times. (22, 28, 34 sts)

Work even until front measures approx 7 (7½, 8) inches from beg, ending with a RS row.

ARMHOLE SHAPING
Next row (WS): Bind off 4 sts, work in pat across. (18, 24, 30 sts)

Work even in pat until armhole measures approx 2 (2¼, 2½) inches from underarm, ending with a WS row.

NECK SHAPING
Work in pat across first 6 (9, 11) sts and place sts on holder, work in pat to end of row. (12, 15, 19 sts)

Continuing in pat, dec 1 st at neck edge (k1, ssk) [every RS row] 3 (3, 5) times, then work even on rem 9 (12, 14) sts until front measures same as back to shoulder. Place sts on holder.

LEFT FRONT
Cast on 23 (29, 35) sts and work as for right front to side shaping.

SIDE SHAPING
Beg on next row and maintaining established pat, dec 1 st at beg of row (k1, ssk) [every 8th row] 3 times. (22, 28, 34 sts)

Work even in pat until front measures approx 7 (7½, 8) inches from beg, ending with a WS row.

ARMHOLE SHAPING
Next row (WS): Bind off 4 sts, work in pat across. (18, 24, 30 sts)

Work even in pat until armhole measures approx 2 (2¼, 2½) inches from underarm, ending with a WS row.
Next row (RS): Work in pat to last 6 (9, 11) sts. Place these sts on a holder. (12, 15, 19 sts)

NECK SHAPING
Continue to work in pat, dec 1 st at neck edge (knit to last 3 sts, k2tog, k1) [every RS row] 3 (3, 5) times, then work even on rem 9 (12, 14) sts until front measures same as back to shoulder. Place sts on holder.

SLEEVES
BORDER
Cast on 23 (25, 29) sts.

Beg with a WS row, knit 6 rows (3 ridges of garter st); inc 6 (4, 6) sts evenly across last row. (29, 29, 35 sts)

Purl 1 row, knit 1 row.

BODY
Row 1 (WS): P1, k3, *p3, k3; rep from * to last st, end p1.
Row 2: K1, p1, k1B, p1, *k3, p1, k1B, p1; rep from * to last st, end k1.
Row 3: Purl.
Row 4: K1, M1, knit to last st, M1, k1. (31, 31, 37 sts)

Work Rows 5–8 of Little Bows pat.

Continuing in pat as established, inc 1 st at each edge [every 8th row] 1 (2, 2) time(s), working inc sts in St st. (33, 35, 41 sts)

Work even in pat until sleeve measures 6 (7, 8) inches or desired length to underarm.

Mark each end of last row, then work even for approx ¾ inch more, ending with Row 4 or 8.

Bind off knitwise on WS.

ASSEMBLY
Bind off front and back shoulders tog, using 3-needle bind off.

FRONT BAND
Notes: A circular needle is recommended to accommodate the sts more easily; do not join, work back and forth in rows.

For boy, make buttonhole on left front instead of right front.

With RS facing, beg at lower right-front corner, pick up and knit 3 sts across end of lower border, 2 sts for every 3 rows along front edge to neck, place marker, M1, k6 (9, 11) sts from holder, place marker, pick up and knit 7 (8, 9) sts along neck edge, k17 (17, 19) back neck sts from holder, pick up and knit 7 (8, 9) sts along left neck edge, place marker, k6 (9, 11) sts from holder, M1, place marker, pick up and knit sts along left-front edge to match right edge, end with 3 sts across lower border.

Row 1 (WS): Sl 1, knit across.
Row 2 (RS): Sl 1, knit to first marker, yo (buttonhole), sl marker, k1, M1, knit to 1 st before next marker, knit next 2 sts tog, replacing marker after resulting st, knit to 1 st before next marker, *at the same time,* dec 2 sts across back neck, knit next 2 sts tog, replacing marker before resulting st, knit to 1 st before last marker, M1, k1, M1, knit to end.
Row 3: Rep Row 1.
Row 4: Sl 1, knit to first marker, M1, sl marker, k1, M1, knit to 1 st before next marker, knit next 2 sts tog, replacing marker after resulting st, knit to 1 st before next marker, knit next 2 sts tog, replacing marker before resulting st, knit to 1 st before last marker, M1, k1, M1, knit to end.
Row 5: Rep Row 1.
Bind off all sts purlwise on RS.

FINISHING
Sew sleeve tops into armholes; match markers to sides of body and sew sleeve edges to bound-off sts of body. Sew sleeve and body seams.

Sew button on left-front band to match buttonhole.

Block lightly.

CUBE IN FEATURED YARN

CUBE PANEL
MAKE 1 OF EACH COLOR
Cast on 22 sts.
Rows 1 (RS)–42: Knit. (21 ridges)
Next row: Purl. Mark each end with a scrap of contrasting yarn or small pin for corners.
Next row: Knit, inc 1 st. (23 sts)
Beg with a knit row, work 3 rows in St st.
Work [Rows 1–8 of Little Bows pat for cube] 3 times.
Next row (WS): Knit, dec 1 st. (22 sts)
Bind off purlwise on RS.

ASSEMBLY
With B, overcast sts in next to last garter ridge in middle of each panel, then sew panels into a cube using overcast or desired st, matching corner markers, and leaving approx 3 inches of last edge open. Stuff to desired firmness, complete seam and fasten off securely.

CUBE IN OPTION YARN

With size 9 (5.5mm) needles, work pieces as for featured cube.

Felt each piece by hand or machine, following the basic felting instructions on page 173 until piece measures approx 4¼ x 8½ inches.

Assemble as for cube in featured yarn, using A to sew overcast seams. ∎

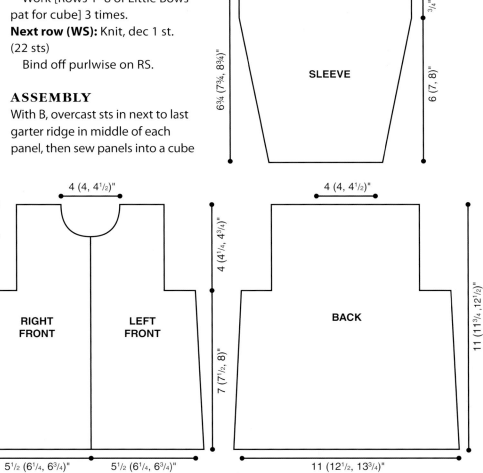

Sure-Bet Gifts & More

Look here for gift ideas that are splendid—never mundane! We've included wearable accessories like a wrap, scarf, belt, socks, fingerless gloves and hats. You'll also find a place mat, tea cozy, kitchen set, felted hangers and even a dog coat.

Memory Book Cover

A simple binder becomes a special photo keeper with the addition of an easy-to-knit cover. It's great for using up scraps of yarn too!

Design by Celeste Pinheiro

SKILL LEVEL
■■□□ EASY

FINISHED SIZE
Fits 1- and 1½-inch-thick binders

MATERIALS
- **Featured yarn:** TLC Cotton Plus 51 percent cotton/49 percent acrylic worsted weight yarn (178 yds/100g per ball): 1 ball each lavender #3590 (A), mint #3645 (B), yellow #3222 (C), turquoise #3667 (D)

- **Option yarn:** Red Heart Super Saver 100 percent acrylic worsted weight yarn (364 yds/198g per skein): 1 skein each medium thyme #406 (A), gold #321 (B), linen #330 (C), carrot #256 (D)
- Size 7 (4.5mm) straight needles or size needed to obtain gauge
- Tapestry needle

GAUGE
18 sts and 26 rows = 4 inches/10cm in St st
  To save time, take time to check gauge.

PATTERN STITCH
Stripe Pat (odd number of sts)
Row 1 (RS): With A, purl.
Rows 2 and 3: With A, work in St st.
Row 4: P1 A, *p1 D, p1 A; rep from * across.
Rows 5 and 6: With A, work in St st.
Rows 7 and 8: With B, purl.
Rows 9 and 10: With C, work in St st.
Row 11: K1 D, *k1 C, k1 D; rep from * across.
Row 12: P1 D, *p1 C, p1 D; rep from * across.
Row 13: With D, knit.

Row 14: With A, knit.
Rows 15–19: With A, work in St st.
Rows 20 and 21: With D, knit.
Rows 22–24: With C, work in St st.
Row 25: K1 C, *k1 B, k1 C; rep from * across.
Row 26: With B, purl.
  Rep Rows 1–26 for pat.

COVER
INSIDE FRONT FLAP
With B, cast on 51 sts.
  Knit 3 rows, then work in St st until piece measures 9½ inches from beg, ending with a WS row.

BODY
Work [Rows 1–26 of Stripe pat] twice, then rep Rows 1–20.
  With D, work in St st for 9½ inches.

INSIDE BACK FLAP
With B, work in St st for 9½ inches.
  Knit 4 rows.
  Bind off.

FINISHING
Sew tops and bottoms of flaps to body.
  Sl over notebook. ∎

Option

Sporty Tea Cozy

Our featured tea cozy is reminiscent of the everyday work sock—perfect for the manly man—while our more feminine version sports a bright pink color and a pompom.

Designs by Katharine Hunt

SKILL LEVEL

■■■□ INTERMEDIATE

FINISHED SIZE

Fits 4 (6) cup "Brown Betty"-style teapot Instructions are given for smaller size, with larger size in parentheses. When only 1 number is given, it applies to both sizes.

Option

MATERIALS

- **Featured yarn (work-sock version):** Plymouth Galway Worsted 100 percent wool worsted weight yarn (210 yds/100g per ball): 1 ball each gray heather #702 (A), natural #1 (B) and red #44 (C)

[4 MEDIUM]

- **Option yarn (pink version):** Plymouth Encore Worsted 75 percent acrylic/25 percent wool worsted weight yarn (200 yds/100g per ball): 1 ball each pink #137 (A), ecru #256 (B), light green #3335 (C)
- Size 10 (6mm) double-pointed needles (set of 4)
- Size 10½ (6.5mm) 16-inch (24-inch) circular needle or size needed to obtain gauge
- Stitch holders
- Tapestry needle

GAUGE

18 sts and 20 rows = 4 inches/10cm over K3, P1 Rib (unblocked and unstretched) with larger needles and 2 strands held tog
   To save time, take time to check gauge.

PATTERN STITCH

K3, P1 Rib (multiple of 4 sts)
Row/Rnd 1 (RS): *K3, p1; rep from * to end.
Row/Rnd 2: Knit the knit sts and purl the purl sts as they appear.
   Rep Row/Rnd 2 for pat.

PATTERN NOTES

This cozy is worked in the round using 2 strands held tog throughout. For work-sock version, Color A = 1 strand each gray heather and natural, Color B = 2 strands red, Color C = 2 strands natural.

Change to dpns when sts no longer fit comfortably on circular needle.

If your teapot's shape is different from the typical round-bowl Brown Betty, check the height of its handle and spout, and if necessary, adjust the position of the side slits. You can also make your cozy taller by working extra rows before the top shaping.

COZY

With circular needle and 2 strands B held tog, cast on

80 (92) sts. Place marker for beg of rnd and join without twisting sts.

Work 2 rnds in K3, P1 Rib.

Pink version only: Work stripes in Rib as follows: 2 rnds A, 2 rnds C, 2 rnds B.

Both versions: Change to A and continue in Rib.

OPEN SIDE SLITS

At the same time, when piece measures 1 (1¾) inches from beg, ending with a WS row, make side slits as follows:

Next row (RS): Ssk, work 37 (43) sts in rib, k1; sl rem 40 (46) sts to holder, turn.

Next row: K1, work rib as established to last st, k1.

Working back and forth, and knitting first and last sts on every row, work even in pat as established until piece measures 5 (6½) inches, ending with a WS row. Put on holder.

Join yarn and rep on other side.

CLOSE SIDE SLITS

Next rnd: Resume working in the round, joining pieces tog to form slits. (78, 90 sts)

Dec rnd: Dec evenly around as follows: Work [k1, k2tog] above each set of k3 sts, and k2 over each side slit. (60, 69 sts)

SHAPE TOP (4-CUP SIZE ONLY):

Rnd 1: *K2, p1; rep from * around.

Rnd 2: *K2tog, p1; rep from * around. (40 sts)

Rnd 3: *K1, p1; rep from * around.

Rnd 4: With C, *k1, p1; rep from * around.

Rnd 5: Knit.

Rnd 6: *K2tog; rep from * around. (20 sts)

Rnd 7: With B, knit.

Rnd 8: *K2tog; rep from* around. (10 sts)

Rnd 9: Knit.

Cut yarn, leaving a 6-inch tail.

Using tapestry needle, thread tail through rem sts and pull tight.

SHAPE TOP (6-CUP SIZE ONLY):

Rnds 1 and 2: With B, *k2, p1; rep from * around.

Rnd 3: With C, *k2tog, p1; rep from * around. (46 sts)

Rnd 4: *K1, p1; rep from * around.

Rnd 5: With A, knit.

Rnd 6: *K2tog; rep from * around. (23 sts)

Rnds 7 and 8: With B, knit.

Rnd 9: *K2tog, k1; rep from * to last 2 sts, k2tog. (15 sts)

Rnd 10: *K1, k2tog; rep from * around. (10 sts)

Cut yarn, leaving a 6-inch tail.

Using tapestry needle, thread tail through rem sts and pull tight.

FINISHING

Weave in ends.

POMPOM (PINK VERSION ONLY)

Cut 2 cardboard circles approx 1 inch in diameter. Cut a hole in the center of each circle, about ½-inch in diameter. Thread a tapestry needle with 2 strands of C. Holding both circles tog, insert needle through center hole, over the outside edge, through center again until entire circle is covered and center hole is filled (thread more length of yarn as needed).

With sharp scissors, cut yarn between the 2 circles all around the circumference.

Using two 12-inch strands of yarn, sl yarn between circles and overlap yarn ends 2 or 3 times to prevent knot from slipping, pull tightly and tie into a firm knot. Remove cardboard and fluff out pompom by rolling it between your hands. Trim even with scissors, leaving tying ends for attaching pompom to cozy.

Sew pompom to top of cozy. ■

Alluring Shawl

Add buttons to this shawl to keep it in place right where you want it to stay. Change the yarn choice and create a completely different look.

Design by Bobbie Matela

SKILL LEVEL
 EASY

FINISHED SIZE
20 x 54 inches

MATERIALS
- **Featured yarn:** Moda Dea Beadnik 90 percent acrylic/5 percent polyester/5 percent PVC worsted weight yarn (103 yds/50g per ball): 6 balls grove green #2917
- **Option yarn:** Twilleys of Stamford Freedom Spirit 100 percent wool worsted weight yarn (131 yds/ 50g per ball): 5 balls force #503
- Size 8 (5mm) knitting needles or size needed to obtain gauge
- 2 decorator buttons (shown with #P39105/94 cinnamon stick from Buttons Etc.)

GAUGE
14 sts and 28 rows = 4 inches/10cm in garter st.
  To save time, take time to check gauge.

SPECIAL ABBREVIATION
Kw2 (knit wrapping twice): Knit next st, wrapping yarn twice around needle.

Feature

INSTRUCTIONS

Cast on 80 sts.

Rows 1–6: Knit.

Row 7: K1, *kw2; rep from * to last st, k1.

Row 8: K1, *knit, dropping extra wrap; rep from * to last st, k1.

Rep Rows 1–8 until piece measures approx 53 inches.

Rep Rows 1–6.

Bind off all sts.

FINISHING

Block to open st pat.

Weave in all ends.

Referring to photo for placement, sew buttons to left front of shawl. Use yarn wraps for buttonholes. ■

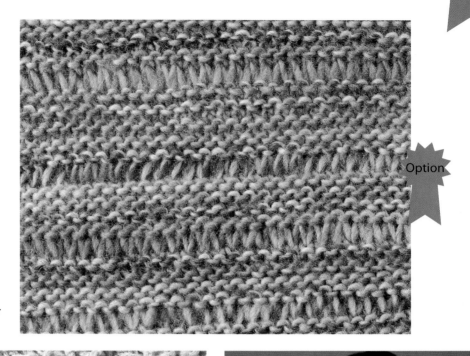

Option

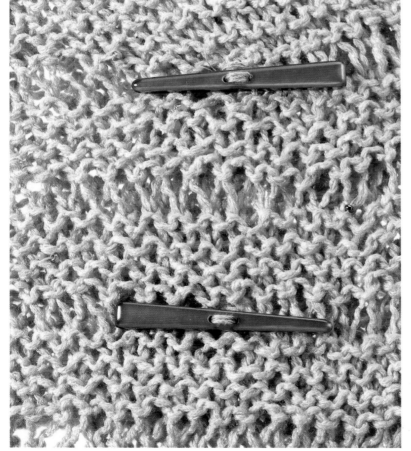

Handy Hostess Set

Dishcloth and towel topper will provide unexpected pleasure to their recipient. Make them to match the kitchen decor for a thoughtful gift.

Designs by Kathy Wesley

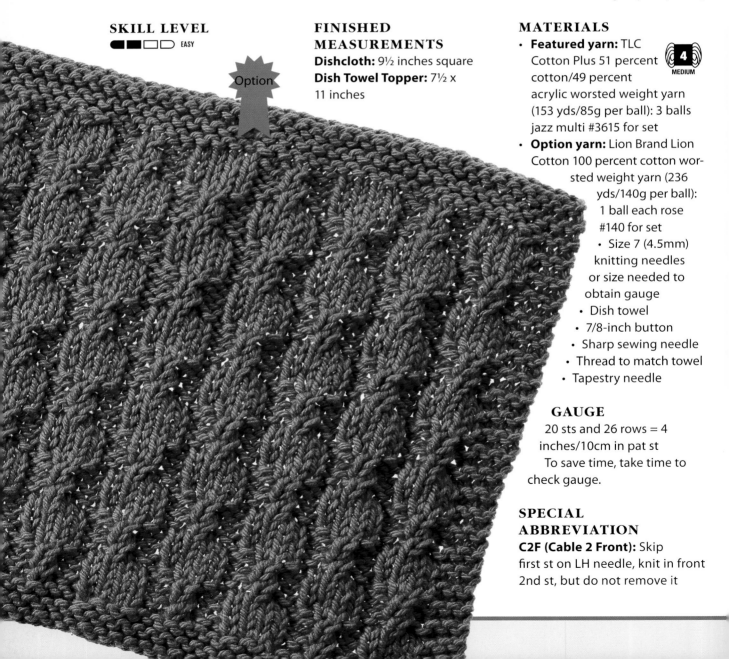

SKILL LEVEL
■■□□ EASY

Option

FINISHED MEASUREMENTS
Dishcloth: 9½ inches square
Dish Towel Topper: 7½ x 11 inches

MATERIALS
- **Featured yarn:** TLC Cotton Plus 51 percent cotton/49 percent acrylic worsted weight yarn (153 yds/85g per ball): 3 balls jazz multi #3615 for set
- **Option yarn:** Lion Brand Lion Cotton 100 percent cotton worsted weight yarn (236 yds/140g per ball): 1 ball each rose #140 for set
  - Size 7 (4.5mm) knitting needles or size needed to obtain gauge
  - Dish towel
  - 7/8-inch button
  - Sharp sewing needle
  - Thread to match towel
- Tapestry needle

4 MEDIUM

GAUGE
20 sts and 26 rows = 4 inches/10cm in pat st
To save time, take time to check gauge.

SPECIAL ABBREVIATION
C2F (Cable 2 Front): Skip first st on LH needle, knit in front 2nd st, but do not remove it

Feature

from needle, then knit in first st and sl both sts off needle.

PATTERN STITCH
(multiple of 10 sts + 4)

Rows 1 and 3 (WS): P1, *p3, k2, p2, k2, p1; rep from * to last 3 sts, p3.

Rows 2 and 4 (RS): K3, *k1, p2, C2F, p2, k3; rep from * to last st, k1.

Rows 5 and 7: K1, *p2, k2, p4, k2; rep from * to last 3 sts, p2, k1.

Rows 6 and 8: P1, C2F, *p2, k4, p2, C2F; rep from * to last st, p1.
    Rep Rows 1–8 for pat.

PATTERN NOTE
A chart for the pat is included for those preferring to work from charts.

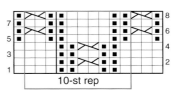

HANDY HOSTESS SET

STITCH KEY
■ P on RS, k on WS
□ K on RS, p on WS
⧓ C2F

DISHCLOTH
Long-tail cast on 46 sts.

BORDER
Knit 4 rows.
Next row (RS): Knit and inc 4 sts evenly spaced across. (50 sts)

BODY
Row 1 (WS): K3, work in pat to last 3 sts, k3.

Maintaining 3-st garter edge, continue in pat as established until piece measures approx 8¾ inches, ending with Row 4.

BORDER
Next row: Knit, dec 4 sts evenly spaced across. (46 sts)
Knit 4 rows.
Bind off knitwise.
Weave in ends.
Block to finished measurements.

TOWEL TOPPER
Long-tail cast on 36 sts.

BORDER
Knit 2 rows.
Next row (RS): Knit, inc 2 sts evenly spaced across. (38 sts)

BODY
Row 1 (WS): K2, work in pat to last 2 sts, k2.

Maintaining 2-st garter edge, work Rows 2–5 of pat.

Row 6 (dec row): K2, ssk, work in pat as established to last 4 sts, k2tog, k2. (36 sts)

Rep dec row [every 4th row] 9 times more. (18 sts)

Work even for 7 rows, ending with a WS row.

BUTTON FLAP
Note: RS of body is now WS for flap.

Maintaining 2-st garter edge, work Rows 1–8 of pat.

Rep Rows 1–5.

Next row (buttonhole row): K2, p1, C2F, p2, k1, bind off 2 sts, k1, p2, C2F, p1, k2.

Next row: Work in pat across, and using backward lp method, cast on 2 sts over bound-off sts.

Next row: K2, p1, C2F, p2, k4, p2, C2F, p1, k2.

Rep Rows 1–4.

Knit 2 rows.

Bind off knitwise.

FINISHING
Weave in ends.

Block to finished measurements.

With sharp needle and thread, sew to edge of dish towel, gathering towel fabric as necessary.

Fold over button flap and sew on button opposite buttonhole. ∎

Cool Felted Hangers

Clothes won't slip off these neat felted hangers. They're so quick and easy you'll want to make them in a rainbow of colors.

Design by Sara Louise Harper

SKILL LEVEL
 EASY

FINISHED SIZE
Fits standard wooden coat/shirt hanger 16–19 inches wide

MATERIALS

- **Featured yarn:** Plymouth Galway Worsted 100 percent wool worsted weight yarn (210 yds/100g per ball): 1 ball each green #146, pink #135 and blue green #111 (set of 3 hanger covers)
- **Option yarn:** Moda Dea Eclipse 60 percent extra-fine wool/40 percent nylon worsted weight yarn (125 yds/50g per ball): 1 ball linen #2551 (1 hanger cover)
- Size 8 (5mm) circular needle or size needed to obtain gauge
- Tapestry needle
- Polyester fiberfill (if desired)
- Wooden hangers

PRE-FELTED GAUGE
20 sts and 24 rows = 4 inches/ 10 cm in St st before felting
   Gauge is not critical to this project.

SPECIAL ABBREVIATION
W&T (Wrap and Turn): With yarn on WS, sl next st purlwise, bring yarn to RS between needles, sl same st back to LH needle, bring yarn to WS between needles, turn work.

SPECIAL TECHNIQUE
Hiding short-row wraps: On RS, knit to st just before wrapped st, insert the needle under wrap

Option

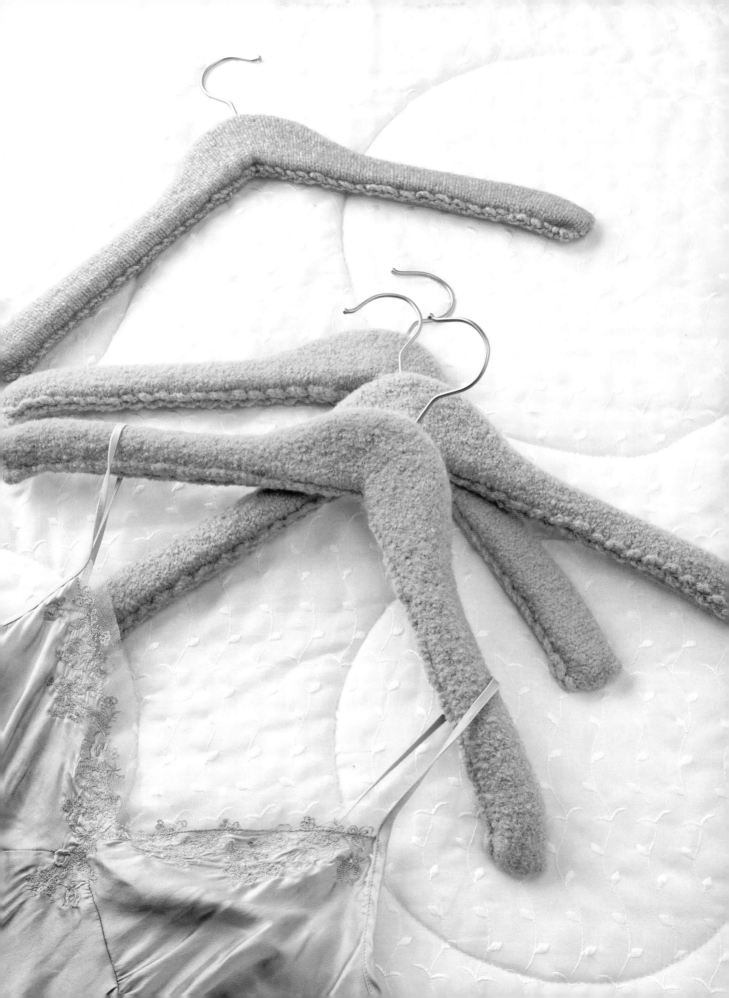

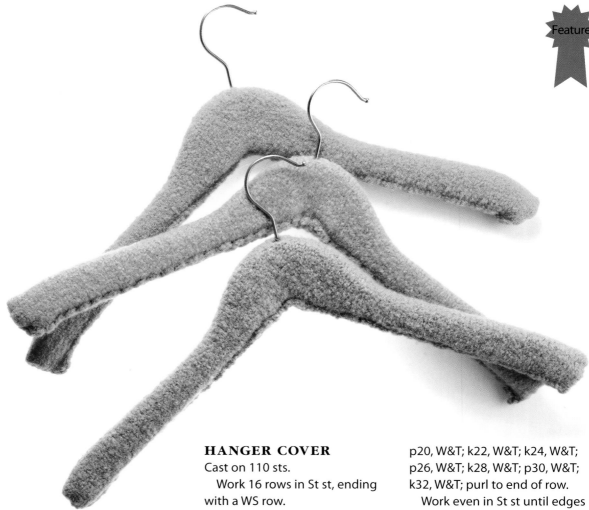

Feature

and knitwise into st and knit st and wrap tog; on WS, purl to st just before wrapped st, insert the right needle from behind into back lp of wrap and place it on left needle then purl wrap and st tog.

PATTERN NOTES

Pat is worked back and forth; a circular needle is used to accommodate the large number of sts.

This pat utilizes short rows.

HANGER COVER

Cast on 110 sts.

Work 16 rows in St st, ending with a WS row.

Next row: Continue in St st and beg working short rows as follows: K70, W&T; p30, W&T; k28, W&T; p26, W&T; k24, W&T; p22, W&T; k20, W&T; p18, W&T.

Next row: Knit to end, hiding wraps as you come to them.

Next row: Purl, hiding rem wraps.

Next row (RS): K54, bind off next 2 sts (opening for top of hanger), then knit to end.

Next row: Purl across, casting on 2 sts over the bound-off sts.

Next row: Beg working short rows as follows, hiding wraps as you come to them: k64, W&T;

p20, W&T; k22, W&T; k24, W&T; p26, W&T; k28, W&T; p30, W&T; k32, W&T; purl to end of row.

Work even in St st until edges measure 5½ inches.

Bind off.

FINISHING

Place a few safety pins in top opening so that it does not fully close during felting process. Follow basic felting instructions on page 173 until piece is desired size to fit over hanger.

Remove pins, then sl cover on hanger and close bottom edge by working a whipstitch or a running st; for added softness (if desired), stuff with fiberfill before completely closing. Allow to dry completely. ∎

Intriguing Shadows Place Mats

This easy place mat is fun for exploring color without having to make color changes in the middle of the row. The optical illusion will entertain dinner guests.

Design by Julie Gaddy

SKILL LEVEL

 EASY

FINISHED SIZE

Approx 18 x 13½ inches
(excluding fringe)

MATERIALS

- **Featured yarn**: Moda Dea Washable Wool 100 percent merino wool superwash worsted weight yarn (166 yds/100g per ball): 1 ball each plum #4431 (MC) and raspberry #4474 (CC)
- **Option yarn:** TLC Cotton Plus 51 percent cotton/40 percent acrylic worsted weight yarn (178 yds/100g per ball): 1 ball each periwinkle #3533 (MC) and tangerine #3252 (CC)
- Size 8 (5mm) knitting needles or size needed to obtain gauge

GAUGE

23 sts and 46 rows = 4 inches/10cm in garter st
   To save time, take time to check gauge.

Option

PATTERN NOTES

The colors alternate every 2 rows, with changes always taking place on RS rows.

RS rows are knit across with the new color and WS rows are worked in pattern.

Do not cut yarn when changing colors—just let the color not in use float along the selvage.

PLACE MAT

Using MC and long-tail method, cast on 85 sts.

Knit 9 rows (5 garter ridges).

Beg pat st

Row 1 (RS): With MC, knit.

Row 2 (WS): With MC, knit 10, p1, k63, p1, k10.

Row 3 (RS): With CC, knit.

Row 4 (WS): With CC, k12, p61, k12.

Continue working in this manner, alternating the colors and knitting across on all RS rows and working patterned WS rows as follows:

Row 6: With MC, k10, p3, k59, p3, k10.

Row 8: With CC, k14, p57, k14.

Row 10: With MC, k10, p5, k55, p5, k10.

Row 12: With CC, k16, p53, k16.

Row 14: With MC, k10, p7, k51, p7, k10.

Row 16: With CC, k18, p49, k18.

Row 18: With MC, k10, p9, k47, p9, k10.

Row 20: With CC, k20, p45, k20.

Row 22: With MC, k10, p11, k43, p11, k10.

Row 24: With CC, k22, p41, k22.

Row 26: With MC, k10, p13, k39, p13, k10.

Row 28: With CC, k24, p37, k24.

Row 30: With MC, k10, p15, k35, p15, k10.

Row 32: With CC, k26, p33, k26.

Row 34: With MC, k10, p17, k31, p17, k10.

Row 36: With CC, k28, p29, k28.

Row 38: With MC, k10, p19, k27, p19, k10.

Row 40: With CC, k30, p25, k30.

Row 42: With MC, k10, p21, k23, p21, k10.

Row 44: With CC, k32, p21, k32.

Row 46: With MC, k10, p23, k19, p23, k10.

Row 48: With CC, k34, p17, k34.

Row 50: With MC, k10, p25, k15, p25, k10.

Rows 52–98: Rep Rows 48–2, making a mirrored image.

With MC, knit 10 rows.

Next row: K5, bind off knitwise to last 5 sts, k5.

FRINGE

Remove needle from work and make fringe as follows:

Unravel the 5 sts on each edge (for ease in working, only unravel a few rows at a time). Using overhand knot, knot each row of fringe near the base to form a stable edge. On the edge where the color changes occur, you will have to clip the lp in the fringe end before you tie the knots, because each row will have 1 strand of MC and 1 strand of CC tied tog in the fringe.

FINISHING

Block place mat to finished measurements.

Trim fringe even. ■

Fun & Felted Bag

Carry this tote with your current knitting project or use it every day. This felted wool knit will last a lot longer than the typical purchased tote.

Design by Sara Louise Harper

SKILL LEVEL
■■□□ **EASY**

FINISHED SIZE
Approx 15 x 14 x 5½ inches, after felting

MATERIALS
- **Featured yarn:** Knit One, Crochet Too Paint Box 100 percent wool worsted weight yarn (100 yds/50g per ball): 2 balls thistle #01 (A) and 3 balls pansy #16 (B)
- **Option yarn:** Universal Yarn Inc. Deluxe Worsted 100% Wool 100 percent wool worsted weight yarn (220 yds/100g per skein): 2 skeins light blue-green #71662
- Size 7 (4.5 mm) 24-inch circular needle or size needed to obtain gauge
- Four colorful buttons, any size
- Sewing needle and coordinating thread
- Hook-and-loop tape (optional)

4 MEDIUM

PRE-FELTED GAUGE
19 sts and 26 rows = 4 inches/10 cm in St st

To save time, take time to check gauge.

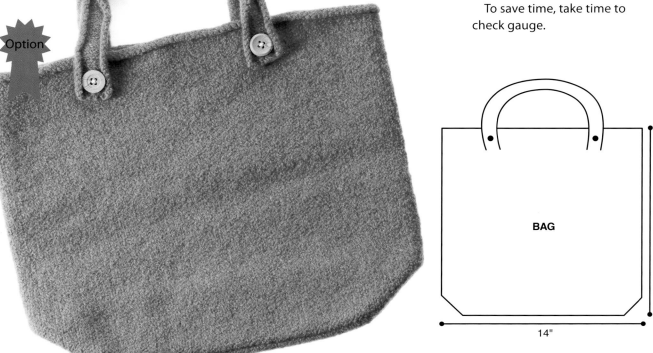

Option

BAG

15"

14"

PATTERN NOTE

Instructions are given for bag in Featured Yarn. Bag in Option Yarn is worked in single color following same pat, but disregarding color changes.

BASE

Using B and beg with fuchsia/ purple area of yarn, cast on 50 sts.

Work in St st for 6 inches, then bind off.

SIDES

With RS of base facing, pick up and knit 48 sts along the long sides and 25 sts along the short sides; place marker for beg of rnd and join. (146 sts)

Work in St st until sides measure 7 inches.

Change to A; continue in St st until sides measure 17 inches.

Work 2 rnds in fuchsia/purple area of B.

Bind off all sts.

HANDLES
Make 2

Using fuchsia/purple area of B, cast on 75 sts.

Work 10 rows in St st.

Bind off all sts.

FINISHING

Weave in all loose ends.

Felt pieces separately following basic felting instructions on page 173

until finished measurements are obtained or pieces are desired size.

Pin handles flat. Lay tote flat and allow base to collapse inside the bag as shown on schematic sketch. When completely dry, attach handles to outside of bag by sewing colorful buttons through fabric of both bag and strap. Attach hook-and-loop tape at each side of center top for closure (optional). ∎

Not-So-Square Hat & Scarf Set

The modular mitered-square design gives this set a funky geometric style that appeals to the eye, while at the same time providing a bit of fun.

Designs by Christine L. Walter

SKILL LEVEL
 INTERMEDIATE

FINISHED MEASUREMENTS
Hat: Fits head circumference of 20–22 inches
Scarf: Approx 60 x 7 inches

MATERIALS
- **Featured yarn:** Plymouth Boku 95 percent wool/5 percent silk worsted weight yarn (99 yds/50g per ball): 3 balls orange/pink/brown #9 (MC) for set

4 MEDIUM

- **Featured yarn:** Plymouth Galway 100 percent wool worsted weight yarn (210 yds/100g per ball): 2 balls dark green #703 (CC) for set
- **Option yarn:** Moda Dea Fashionista 50 percent acrylic/50 percent Tencel/Lyocell worsted weight yarn (183 yds/100g per ball): 2 balls each of sand castle #6117 (MC) and milk chocolate #6140 (CC) for set
- Size 8 (5mm) 16-inch circular needle and set of double-pointed needles (hat) and 24-inch or longer circular needle (scarf) or size needed to obtain gauge
- Size 10 (6mm) double-pointed needles
- Stitch markers
- Stitch holders
- Tapestry needle

GAUGE
1 mitered square = 3 inches/7.5cm square
   To save time, take time to check gauge.

SPECIAL ABBREVIATIONS
M1 (Make 1): Insert LH needle from front to back under the horizontal lp between the last st worked and next st on left needle. With RH needle, knit into the back of this lp.
MB (Make Bobble): Knit into front and back of st twice then knit into front once more (5 sts), turn, k5, turn, p5, turn, k5, turn, sl 2nd, 3rd, 4th, and 5th sts over the first st, k1.

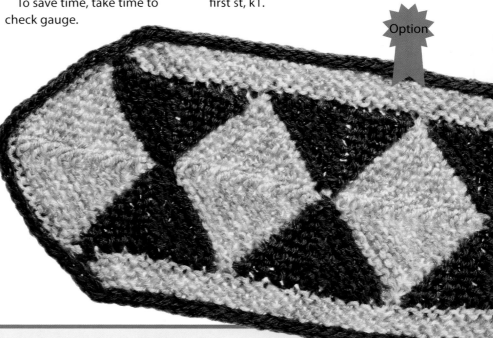

Option

PATTERN NOTES

Hat and scarf are constructed using mitered squares that are joined by half squares. The squares in the scarf are lined up end to end from cast on to bind off from the center out. The squares in the hat are lined up side by side with cast-on edges all pointing upwards toward the crown.

Sl last st of each row purlwise with yarn in front.

SQUARES

Cast on 23 sts using knitted cast on.

Row 1 and all WS rows: K1-tbl, knit to last st, sl 1.

Row 2 (RS): K1-tbl, k9, k3tog-tbl, k9, sl 1. (21 sts)

Row 4: K1-tbl, k8, k3tog-tbl, k8, sl 1. (19 sts)

Row 6: K1-tbl, k7, k3tog-tbl, k7, sl 1. (17 sts)

Row 8: K1-tbl, k6, k3tog-tbl, k6, sl 1. (15 sts)

Row 10: K1-tbl, k5, k3tog-tbl, k5, sl 1. (13 sts)

Row 12: K1-tbl, k4, k3tog-tbl, k4, sl 1. (11 sts)

Row 14: K1-tbl, k3, k3tog-tbl, k3, sl 1. (9 sts)

Row 16: K1-tbl, k2, k3tog-tbl, k2, sl 1. (7 sts)

Row 18: K1-tbl, k1, k3tog-tbl, k1, sl 1. (5 sts)

Row 20: K1-tbl, k3tog-tbl, sl 1. (3 sts)

Row 21: K3tog-tbl. (1 st)

Cut yarn and fasten off.

HALF-SQUARES

Worked over 23 sts picked up along edges of 2 squares.

Rows 1, 3, 5 and 7: K1-tbl, knit

to last st, sl 1.

Row 2 (RS): K1-tbl, k2tog, k7, k3tog-tbl, k7, k2tog, sl 1. (19 sts)

Row 3: K1-tbl, k17, sl 1.

Row 4: K1-tbl, k2tog, k5, k3tog-tbl, k5, k2tog, sl 1. (15 sts)

Row 5: K1-tbl, k13, sl 1.

Row 6: K1-tbl, k2tog, k3, k3tog-tbl, k3, k2tog, sl 1. (11 sts)

Row 7: K1-tbl, k9, sl 1.

Row 8: K1-tbl, k2tog, k1, k3tog-tbl, k1, k2tog, sl 1. (7 sts)

Row 9: K1-tbl, k2tog, k1, k2tog, sl 1. (5 sts)

Row 10: K1-tbl, k3tog-tbl, sl 1. (3 sts)

Row 11: K3tog-tbl. (1 st)

Cut yarn and fasten off.

SCARF

With MC, make 18 squares.

CENTER STRIPE

Join center 2 squares as follows: With CC, pick up and knit 11 sts along right edge of 1 mitered square from cast-on edge to bind off; pick up and knit 1 st through both the tip of current square and tip of 2nd square; pick up and knit 11 sts along left side of 2nd square from cast-on edge to bind-off edge. (23 sts)

Work half-square.

In the same manner, work a 2nd half-square filling in the other side of these 2 squares, forming a hexagon.

Join next square in the same manner, but add each subsequent square so that bind-off edge of next square abuts the center of previous square.

Keep adding a new square

to each end until all 18 squares have been joined with 9 each going out from the center.

Center strip is now completed.

BORDER

With RS facing and using smaller needle and MC, pick up and knit 205 sts along 1 edge.

Rows 1, 3 and 5 (WS): Knit.

Row 2, 4 and 6 (RS): K1, k2tog-tbl, knit to last 3 sts, k2tog, k1. (99 sts)

I-CORD BIND OFF

With WS facing, using larger dpn and CC, cast on 3 sts. *K2, skp, do not turn. Sl 3 sts back to LH needle and rep from * until all sts are bound off. Do not cut yarn and leave 3 sts on holder.

Work Border Rows 1–6 on 2nd side of center panel. Do not cut yarn or bind off.

Sl the 3 CC sts from holder to

larger dpn.

Continue I-cord edge along scarf point as follows: slide sts to end of needle, k3 sts (unattached I-cord, first corner turned); *slide sts to end of needle, k2, sl 1, k1 in garter ridge, psso; rep from * twice more.

Continue repeating from *, knitting into cast-on edge of mitered square until you reach the tip. Work 1 row of unattached I-cord to turn corner, then continue as before until you reach the border sts on the needle.

Work 1 row of unattached I-cord to turn corner, then bind off border sts as on other side.

Work I-cord edge along point as before.

Cut yarn and graft the 2 ends of the I-cord edging.

FINISHING

Weave in ends.
Block lightly.

HAT

With MC, make 5 squares.

Hold squares with cast-on edge facing upwards; with CC, pick up and knit 11 sts along left cast-on edge of first square, pick up and knit 1 st through corners of both first and 2nd squares, pick up and knit 11 sts along right cast-on edge of 2nd square. Work half-square.

Continue in this manner, joining squares with half-squares, then join first and last squares with half-squares to form tube.

Once all 5 squares are joined at the cast-on edges (crown edge), rep for other side (bottom edge).

CROWN

With smaller dpns, pick up and knit 66 sts along crown edge of center strip. Place marker for beg of rnd and join.

*Purl 1 rnd, knit 1 rnd, rep from * once, then purl 1 rnd.
Next rnd: Knit, dec 2 sts evenly around. (64 sts).
Next rnd: *P8, place marker; rep from * around.
Dec rnd: *Knit to 2 sts before marker, k2tog; rep from * around. (56 sts)

Rep dec rnd [every 4th rnd] twice, then [every other rnd] 4 times. (8 sts)

Cut yarn, leaving an 8-inch tail.
Using tapestry needle, thread tail through rem sts, and pull tight.

BRIM

With RS facing and using smaller dpns and MC, pick up and knit 66 sts along bottom edge of hat. Place marker for beg of rnd and join.
Rnds 1, 3, and 5: Purl.
Rnd 2: K5, *M1, k11; rep from * to last 6 sts, M1, k6. (72 sts)
Rnds 4 and 6: Knit.
Rnd 7: With CC, k2, *MB, k5; rep from * to last 4 sts, MB, k3.
Bind off knitwise.

FINISHING

Weave in ends.
Block lightly. ∎

Holey Moley Scarf

This stitch pattern is so intriguing your knitting time will speed by in a flash. Use a favorite shade and wonderful fiber for this interesting design.

Design by Celeste Pinheiro

SKILL LEVEL
 EASY

FINISHED SIZE
Approx 4 x 59 inches

MATERIALS
- **Featured yarn:** Lily Chin Signature Collection Park Avenue Printed 60 percent merino wool/40 percent fine alpaca worsted weight yarn (109 yds/50g per ball): 3 balls green/teal #136
- **Option yarn:** South West Trading Co. Vickie Howell Collection Rock 40 percent Soysilk fibers/30 percent fine wool/30 percent hemp worsted weight yarn (110 yds/50g per ball): 3 balls Shirley #756
- Size 7 (4.5mm) needles or size needed to obtain gauge
- Tapestry needle

GAUGE
25 sts and 50 rows = 4 inches/10cm in garter st

To save time take time to check gauge.

PATTERN STITCH
Hole Stitch (multiple of 8 sts + 1)
Row 1 (WS): Knit.
Rows 2 and 3: Knit.
Row 4: K2, *bind off 5 sts, k3; rep from *, end bind off 5 sts, k2.
Row 5: K2, *cast on 5 sts, k3; rep from *, end cast on 5 sts, k2.
Rows 6 and 7: Knit.
Row 8: K6, *bind off 5 sts, k3; rep from *, end bind off 5 sts, k6.
Row 9: K6, *cast on 5 sts, k3, rep from *, end cast on 5 sts, k6.
Rep Rows 2–9 for pat.

PATTERN NOTE
In Rows 4 and 8, k3 includes 1 st rem from bind-off.

Cast on in Rows 5 and 9 using backward-lp cast on (see Fig. 1).

INSTRUCTIONS
Cut 60 (15-inch) strands; set aside for fringe.

Cast on 25 sts.

Work in pat until piece measures approx 59 inches, ending with Row 7 of pat.

Bind off all sts.

FRINGE
Cut 60 (15-inch) strands. Using 10 strands for each knot, *fold 10 strands in half. With RS facing and beg at first hole at 1 end of scarf, use fingers to draw folded end from RS to WS. Pull loose ends through folded section. Draw knot up firmly. Rep from *, placing 2 more knots in 2 other holes on end. Rep at other end. Trim ends even. ■

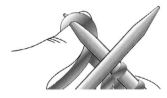

Fig. 1

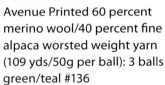

Option

Zigzag Waves

Make this scarf in your choice of widths. Choose a print variegated yarn or change colors for each triangle. Wouldn't a multicolored scrap scarf be fun?

Design by Celeste Pinheiro

SKILL LEVEL

 EASY

FINISHED SIZE

Approx 3½ (6) x 60 inches
Instructions are given for narrower size, with wider size in parentheses. When only 1 number is given, it applies to both sizes.

MATERIALS

- **Featured yarn:**
  Patons SWS 70 percent wool/30 percent soy worsted weight yarn (110 yds/80g per ball): 3 balls natural blue #70128 (wide scarf)
- **Option yarn:** Red Heart Soft Yarn 100 percent acrylic worsted weight yarn (256 yds/140g per ball): 1 ball each cherry red #5142 (A), grape #3729 (B), tangerine #4422 (C) (narrow scarf)
- Size 8 (5mm) knitting needles or size needed to obtain gauge
- Size G/4.00mm crochet hook (for attaching fringe)

GAUGE

16 sts and 32 rows = 4 inches/10cm in garter st
Gauge is not critical to this project.

PATTERN NOTES

Scarf is constructed modularly in triangles.

When casting on, leave 7-inch tails—these will be incorporated into fringe.

In the multicolored scarf, you can use any combination or order of colors, making it a great scrap project; in the sample, triangles were worked in this order:
A, B, C, B.

INSTRUCTIONS

FIRST TRIANGLE

Leaving a 7-inch tail, cast on 24 (30) sts.

Row 1 (WS): Knit.

Row 2 (RS): K2tog, knit to last 2 sts, ssk. (22, 28 sts)

Rep Rows 1 and 2 until 2 sts rem.

Last row: K2tog, then fasten off.

SECOND TRIANGLE

Pick up 24 (30) sts along right edge of first triangle.

Work as for first triangle.

THIRD TRIANGLE

Pick up 24 (30) sts along left edge of 2nd triangle.

Work as for first triangle.

Continue working triangles in this manner, picking up alternately along right and left edges for each succeeding triangle, until piece measures approx 60 inches.

FRINGE

Cut 3 strands each approx 13 inches long for each knot.

Using crochet hook, attach fringe at each corner, then on sides at points where triangles abut (see photo); pull tails through fringe knots. ■

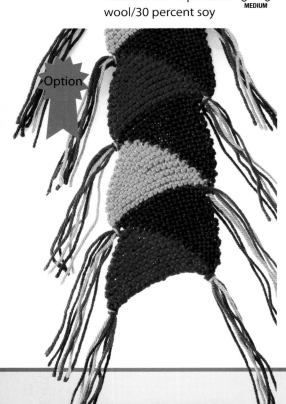

Option

Simple Cables Set

This hat and fingerless glove set has a pair of interesting cables that run along the hand and repeat around the hat.

Designs by Nazanin S. Fard

SKILL LEVEL
■■□□ EASY

FINISHED SIZES
Hat: Fits adult average
Fingerless Gloves: Fits woman's average

MATERIALS
- **Featured yarn:** Moda Dea Washable Wool 100 percent merino wool superwash worsted weight yarn (166 yd/100g per ball): 2 balls tangerine #4453 for set

- **Option yarn:** Moda Dea Eclipse 60 percent extra-fine wool/40 percent nylon worsted weight yarn (125 yds/50g per ball): 3 balls peri #2595 for set
- Size 8 (5mm) 16-inch circular needle and set of 4 double-pointed needles or size needed to obtain gauge
- Stitch markers
- Cable needle
- Tapestry needle

GAUGE
19 sts and 26 rnds = 4 inches/10cm in St st
To save time, take time to check gauge.

SPECIAL ABBREVIATIONS
C6F (Cable 6 Front): Sl 3 sts to cn and hold in front, k3, k3 from cn.
C6B (Cable 6 Back): Sl 3 sts to cn and hold in back, k3, k3 from cn.

PATTERN STITCH
Cable Pat (multiple of 20 sts)
Rnd 1: *K2, (p2, k6) twice, p2; rep from * around.
Rnd 2: *K2, p2, C6F, p2, C6B, p2; rep from * around.
Rnds 3–6: Rep Rnd 1.
Rep Rnds 1–6 for pat.

PATTERN NOTE
Instructions for set in Featured and Option yarn are the same. When working hat, change to dpns when sts no longer fit comfortably on circular needle.

HAT
With circular needle, cast on 120 sts. Place marker for beg of rnd and join without twisting sts.
Work K2, P2 Rib for 3 inches.
Work Cable pat for approx 8 inches or desired length, ending with Rnd 3.

CROWN
Rnd 1: *K2, p2, [k2tog] 3 times, p2tog, [k2tog] 3 times, p2; rep from * around. (78 sts)
Rnd 2: *K2, p2, k3, k2tog, k2, p2; rep from * around. (72 sts)
Rnds 3 and 4: *K2, p2, k6, p2; rep from * around.
Rnd 5: *K2, p2, C6B, p2; rep from * around.
Rnd 6: Rep Rnd 3.
Rnds 7–9: K2tog around. (9 sts)
Cut yarn, leaving a 6-inch tail.
Using tapestry needle, thread tail through rem sts and pull tight.
Weave in all ends.

Option

Next rnd (thumb opening): Work in pat as established for 20 sts, bind off 4 sts, work to end of rnd.

Next rnd: Work in pat as established, casting on 4 sts over bound-off sts.

Work even until piece measures approx 7 inches or desired length, ending with Rnd 3.

Next rnd: *K1, k2tog twice, k1, p2; rep from * once more, then work in pat as established to end of rnd.

Bind off in pat.

LEFT HAND

Work same as Right Hand to thumb opening.

Next rnd (thumb opening): Work in pat as established for 38 sts, bind off 4 sts, work to end of rnd.

Complete as for Right Hand.

FINISHING

Weave in all ends. ■

FINGERLESS GLOVES
RIGHT HAND

Cast on 48 sts.

Distribute evenly on 3 dpns; place marker for beg of rnd and join without twisting sts.

Work K2, P2 Rib for 3 inches.

Set-up Pat

Rnd 1: (K6, p2) twice, k2, p2, k22, p2, k2, p2.

Rnd 2: C6F, p2, C6B, p2, k2, p2, k22, p2, k2, p2.

Rnds 3–6: Rep Rnd 1.

Rep [Rnds 1–6] until piece measures approx 5 inches or desired length to thumb opening.

Warm Their Toes

Keep toes comfy both outside and in the home. You will love these socks for the way they feel inside your boots, or when you wear them around the house instead of slippers.

Design by Susan Robicheau

SKILL LEVEL

■■■□ INTERMEDIATE

FINISHED SIZES

Woman's large (man's large) Instructions are given for woman's size (option yarn), with man's size (featured yarn) in parentheses. When only 1 number is given, it applies to both sizes.

FINISHED MEASUREMENTS

Approx 8 (9¼) inches in circumference

MATERIALS

- **Featured yarn:** Patons Classic Merino Wool 100 percent wool worsted weight yarn (223 yds/100g per ball): 2 balls blue storm #00215 (man's version)
- **Option yarn:** Plymouth Baby Alpaca Worsted Glow 97 percent baby alpaca/3 percent Stellina worsted weight yarn (102 yds/50g per ball): 4 balls olive #3843 (woman's version)
- Size 3 (3.25mm) double-pointed needles (set of 5) or size needed to obtain gauge

Option

- Stitch marker
- Tapestry needle

GAUGE
24 sts and 36 rows = 4 inches/10cm in pat st

To save time, take time to check gauge.

SPECIAL ABBREVIATIONS
N1, N2, N3, N4: Needle 1, needle 2, needle 3, needle 4

PATTERN STITCH
Diagonal Broken Rib (multiple of 8 sts)
Rnd 1: *K1, p1, k1, p5; rep from * around.
Rnd 2 and all even numbered rnds: Knit the knit sts and purl the purl sts.
Rnd 3: *K1, p1, k5, p1; rep from * around.
Rnd 5: *K1, p5, k1, p1; rep from * around.
Rnd 7: *K5, p1, k1, p1; rep from * around.
Rnd 9: *P4, k1, p1, k1, p1; rep from * around.
Rnd 11: *K3, p1, k1, p1, k2; rep from * around.
Rnd 13: *P2, k1, p1, k1, p3; rep from * around.
Rnd 15: *K1, p1, k1, p1, k4; rep from * around.
Rnd 16: Rep Rnd 2.

PATTERN NOTE
For smaller-sized socks, go down in needle size for tighter gauge; more tightly knit socks will last longer.

SOCKS
CUFF
Cast on 48 (56) sts. Divide sts evenly on 4 needles (N1: heel, N2 and N3: instep, N4: heel). Place marker for beg of rnd and join without twisting.

Work in k1, p1 rib for 2 (2½) inches.

LEG
Work 4 reps of Diagonal Broken Rib, ending last rnd on N3 [i.e 12 (14) sts short of beg of rnd].

Sl sts from N4 to N1 for flap.

HEEL FLAP
(worked on N1 only)
Row 1 (RS): K24 (28).
Row 2 (WS): K1, p10 (12), p2tog, p10 (12), k1. (23, 27 sts)
Row 3: K1, *sl 1, k1; rep from * to end.
Row 4: K1, purl to last st, k1.

Rep Rows 3 and 4 until heel flap measures 2½ (2¾) inches.

TURN HEEL
Row 1 (RS): K12 (14), ssk, k1, turn.
Row 2: Sl 1, p2, p2tog, p1, turn.
Row 3: Sl 1, k3, ssk, k1, turn.
Row 4: Sl 1, p4, p2tog, p1, turn.
Rows 6–12 (14): Continue in this manner, working 1 more st each row before dec. (13, 15 sts)
Row 13 (15): Sl 1, k12 (14); do not turn.

GUSSET
Rnd 1: With N1, pick up and knit 13 (15) sts along side of heel flap; work in pat as established across N2 and N3; with N4, pick up and knit 13 (15) sts along side of heel flap, then k6 (8) from N1. (63, 73 sts)
Rnd 2: N1: knit to last 3 sts, k2tog, k1; N2 and N3: work in pat; N4: k1, ssk, knit to end of rnd. (61, 71 sts)
Rnd 3: Work even.

Rep [Rnds 2 and 3] 7 (8) times. (47, 55 sts)

FOOT
Work even until foot measures approx 8½ (10) inches from base of heel or approx 1½ (2) inches less than desired length, and on last rnd, dec 1 st at beg of N3. (46, 54 sts)

TOE
Dec rnd: N1: *knit to last 3 sts, k2tog, k1; N2: k1, ssk, knit to end; rep from * on N3 and N4. (42, 50 sts)

Rep dec rnd [every other rnd] 5 (7) times. (22 sts)

Cut yarn leaving a 16-inch tail.

Sl sts from N4 to N1 and from N3 to N2. (11 sts each needle)

Holding N1 and N2 parallel, graft sts tog using Kitchener st (see page 171).

Weave in all ends. ■

Wanderlust Cap

The wavy ribbing of this great hat means that it will accommodate many sizes of heads. Flattering to both men and women, it will make your list of favorite gifts to knit when in a hurry.

Design by Christine L. Walter

SKILL LEVEL
■■□□ EASY

FINISHED SIZES
Fits adult's small (adult's large)

FINISHED MEASUREMENT
Fits head circumference of 18–20 inches (20–22 inches)

MATERIALS
• **Featured yarn:**
Patons Classic Merino Wool 100 percent wool worsted weight yarn (223 yds/100g per ball): 1 ball camel #77023 (large hat)
• **Option yarn:** Plymouth Jeannee 51 percent cotton/49 percent acrylic worsted weight yarn (107 yds/50g per ball) 2 balls dark coral #2 (small hat)
• Size 8 (5mm) 16-inch circular needle and set of double-pointed needles or size needed to obtain gauge (large hat)
• Size 6 (4mm) 16-inch circular and set of double-pointed needles or size needed to obtain gauge (small hat)
• Stitch marker
• Tapestry needle

GAUGE
Small Hat: 23 sts and 32 rnds = 4 inches/10cm in K2, P2 Rib (slightly stretched) using smaller needles
Large Hat: 21 sts and 28 rnds = 4 inches/10cm in K2, P2 Rib (slightly stretched) using larger needles
To save time, take time to check gauge.

PATTERN NOTES
Hat sizes are adjusted by changing needle size and gauge; both sizes use the same number of sts and rnds.

Change to dpns when sts no longer fit comfortably on circular needle.

Wavy Rib pat will be continued to end of crown shaping.

PATTERN STITCHES
A. K2, P2 Rib
Rnd 1: K1, *p2, k2; rep from * ending k1.
Rep Rnd 1 for pat.

B. Wavy Rib (multiple of 16)
Rnds 1, 3, 5 and 7: *K9, p2, k2, p2, k1; rep from * around.
Rnds 2, 4, 6 and 8: *K1, p6, [k2, p2] twice, k1; rep from * around.
Rnds 9, 11, 13 and 15: *K1, p2, k2, p2, k9; rep from * around.
Rnds 10, 12, 14 and 16: *K1, [p2, k2] twice, p6, k1; rep from * around.
Rep Rnds 1–16 for pat.

HAT
Using appropriate-sized needle, cast on 112 sts; place marker

Feature

Option

for beg of rnd and join without twisting sts.

Work 28 rnds in K2, P2 Rib or until cuff is desired length (it will be folded back doubled).

Work 32 rnds of Wavy Rib.

CROWN
Rnd 1: *K9, p2, k2, p1, k2tog; rep from * around. (105 sts)
Rnd 2: *K1, p6, k2, p2, k2, k2tog; rep from * around. (98 sts)
Rnd 3: *K9, p2, k1, k2tog; rep from * around. (91 sts)
Rnd 4: *K1, p6, k2, p2, k2tog; rep from * around. (84 sts)
Rnd 5: *K9, p1, k2tog; rep from * around. (77 sts)
Rnd 6: *K1, p6, k2, k2tog; rep from * around. (70 sts)
Rnd 7: *K8, k2tog; rep from * around. (63 sts)
Rnd 8: *K1, p6, k2tog; rep from * around. (56 sts)
Rnd 9: *K1, p2, k2, p1, k2tog; rep from * around. (49 sts)
Rnd 10: *K1, p2, k2, k2tog; rep from * around. (42 sts)
Rnd 11: *K1, p2, k1, k2tog; rep from * around. (35 sts)
Rnd 12: *K1, p2, k2tog; rep from * around. (28 sts)
Rnd 13: *K1, p1, k2tog; rep from * around. (21 sts)
Rnd 14: *K1, k2tog; rep from * around. (14 sts)
Rnd 15: *K2tog; rep from * around. (7 sts)
Cut yarn, leaving an 8-inch tail.

Using tapestry needle, thread tail through rem sts twice, and pull tight.

FINISHING
Weave in ends. Block hat lightly using steam and let dry. ∎

Perfect Sash

This may be an easy pattern, but you will have fun when asked, "How did you do that?" You'll also like that there is no tedious finishing—when it's done, it's done.

Design by Julie Gaddy

SKILL LEVEL

 INTERMEDIATE

FINISHED MEASUREMENTS

Approx 1½ inches x 45 inches

MATERIALS

- **Featured yarn:** Plymouth Linen Isle 50 percent cotton/30 percent rayon/20 percent linen worsted weight yarn **4 MEDIUM** (86 yds/50g per ball): 1 ball natural #7009
- **Option yarn:** South West Trading Co. Amerah 100 percent silk worsted weight yarn (97 yds/ 50g per ball): 1 ball wisteria #269

Feature

Option

- Size 6 (4mm) knitting needles or size needed to obtain gauge
- Tapestry needle
- Two decorative rings or D rings having at least a 1½-inch inside diameter
- Sewing needle and coordinating thread

GAUGE

23 sts and 46 rows = 4 inches/10cm in garter st
Gauge is not critical to this project.

SPECIAL TECHNIQUES

Provisional Cast On: With crochet hook and waste yarn, make a chain several sts longer than desired cast on. With knitting needle and project yarn, pick up indicated number of sts in the "bumps" on back of chain. When indicated in pat, "unzip" the crochet chain to release the live-st lps.

I-Cord: *K3, do not turn, sl sts back to LH needle; rep from * until cord is desired length.

I-Cord Bind Off: *K2, k2tog-tbl, do not turn. Sl 3 sts back to LH needle and rep from * across row.

SASH

Using the provisional method, cast on 3 sts.
Work I-cord for 7 rows.
Pick up 6 sts along side of I-cord (I-cord cast on), then with working yarn in front, carefully "unzip" the waste yarn from the provisional cast on and arrange the 3 lps on the needle with WS facing you. (12 sts on needle)
The working yarn will be in front between the picked-up sts and the 3 sts slipped onto the end of the needle. When you look at the sts, the first 9 will appear to be knit sts, and the last 3 will appear to be purl sts.
Turn work.
Pat row: Keeping yarn in back and pulling it across back of work to knit the first st, knit to last 3 sts, bring yarn to front and sl 3 purlwise.

Repeat Pat row until sash measures 44½ inches or desired length from cast-on edge. Allow at least 10 inches more than desired waist size (3 inches to attach buckle and at least 8 inches to secure belt).
Work I-cord bind off to last 3 sts. (6 sts rem: 3 sts of the I-cord being used to bind off on the RH needle, and 3 sts of I-cord edging on LH needle).
Hold needles parallel with purl sides of I-cord sts tog. Using Kitchener st (see page 171), carefully graft last 3 sts of I-cord bind off to the 3 sts that form the left edge of the sash.

FINISHING

Weave in all ends and block to finished measurements as desired.
Insert 1 end of sash into the 2 rings and fold back approx 3 inches. Secure rings by sewing folded end to sash body, hiding sts under I-cord on the sash end. ■

Twisted Cable Dog Coat

Make sure your furry friends are taken care of when the temperature falls. This cable classic is rugged enough for large dogs and sophisticated enough for a little princess.

Design by Gayle Bunn

Option

SKILL LEVEL

 INTERMEDIATE

FINISHED SIZES

Fits small (medium, large) dog Instructions are given for smallest size, with larger sizes in parentheses. When only 1 number is given, it applies to all sizes.

FINISHED MEASUREMENTS

Chest: 13 (16, 24) inches
Length (collar to tail): 11 (15½, 22) inches

MATERIALS

- **Featured yarn:** Plymouth Galway Worsted 100 percent wool worsted weight yarn (210 yds/100g per ball): 1 (2, 3) ball(s) pink #135
- **Option yarn:** Bernat Denimstyle 70 percent acrylic/30 percent cotton worsted weight yarn (196 yds/100g per ball): 1 (2, 3) ball(s) rodeo tan #03012
- Size 8 (5mm) straight, circular (at least 29 inches long) and

set of 4 double-pointed needles or size needed to obtain gauge
- Cable needle
- Stitch markers
- Tapestry needle

GAUGE

20 sts and 25 rows = 4 inches/10cm in St st

To save time, take time to check gauge.

SPECIAL ABBREVIATIONS

C8F (Cable 8 Front): Sl next 4 sts to cn and hold in front, k4, then k4 from cn.

M3 (Make 3 sts in 1st): (K1, p1, k1) all in next st. (1 st becomes 3 sts)

PATTERN STITCHES

A. Cable Panel (12-st panel)
Row 1 (RS): P2, k8, p2.
Row 2 and all WS rows: K2, p8, k2.
Row 3: P2, C8F, p2.
Rows 5 and 7: Rep Row 1.
Row 8: Rep Row 2.
Rep Rows 1–8 for Cable Panel.

B. Trinity St (multiple of 4 sts + 2)
Row 1 (RS): Purl.
Row 2: K1, *M3, p3tog; rep from * to last st, k1.
Row 3: Purl.
Row 4: K1, *p3tog, M3; rep from * to last st, k1.
Rep Rows 1–4 for pat.

DOG COAT

NECKBAND

With straight needles, cast on 46 (58, 82) sts.
Row 1 (RS): K2, *p2, k2; rep from * to end of row.
Row 2 (WS): P2, *k2, p2; rep from * to end of row.

Continue in K2, P2 Rib as established until piece measures 3½ (4, 5) inches, ending with a WS row, and inc 4 sts evenly across last row. (50, 62, 86 sts)

BODY

Pat set-up row 1 (RS): K0 (0, 4), p1 (3, 3), work Row 1 of Trinity St across next 18 (22, 30) sts, work Row 1 of Cable Panel across next 12 sts, work Row 1 of Trinity St across next 18 (22, 30) sts, p1 (3, 3), K0 (0, 4).
Pat set-up row 2: P0 (0, 4), k1 (3, 3), work Row 2 of Trinity St across next 18 (22, 30) sts, work Row 2 of Cable Panel across next 12 sts, work Row 2 of Trinity St across next 18 (22, 30) sts, k1 (3, 3), p0 (0, 4).

Continue in pat as established and inc 1 st at each side [every row] 6 (8, 10) times, then [every RS row] 4 (4, 6) times, ending with a WS row and working new sts so that there are 3 rev St sts before first set of Trinity sts and following 2nd set of Trinity sts (that is, 2 more sts in rev St st for Size S), then work all rem incs in St st. (70, 86, 118 sts)

SHAPE LEG OPENINGS

Row 1 (RS): K8 (10, 13), attach a 2nd ball of yarn and bind off next 5 (6, 9) sts, work in pat as established over next 44 (54, 74) sts (including st on needle after bind off), attach a 3rd ball of yarn, bind off next 5 (6, 9) sts, knit to end of row. Working the 3 sections at once with separate balls of yarn and maintaining pat as established, work even for 1½ (2, 2½) inches, ending with a WS row.
Next row (RS): Using 1 ball of yarn, work across in pat as established and cast on 5 (6, 9) sts over both sets of bound-off sts. (70, 86, 118 sts)

Work even in pat until work measures 5½ (7, 10) inches from Neckband, ending with a WS row. Place a marker at each end of last row.

BACK SHAPING

Bind off 7 (10, 12) sts at beg of next 2 rows. (56, 66, 94 sts)

Bind off 3 sts beg next 2 rows, then dec 1 st each side [every RS row] 7 (8, 10) times. (36, 44, 68 sts)

Work even until piece measures 4½ (6½, 10) inches from markers, ending with a WS row.

Bind off 3 (3, 4) sts at beg of next 6 (8, 10) rows.

Bind off rem 18 (20, 28) sts.

BACK EDGING

With RS facing and using circular needle, pick up and knit 37 (49, 65) sts along body from marker to bound-off sts of back, 18 (20, 28) sts across back edge and 37 (49, 65) sts along opposite side of body to marker. (92, 118, 158 sts)

Beg with a WS row, work 5 rows in K2, P2 rib as for Neckband.

Bind off in rib.

LEG EDGING

With RS facing and using dpns, pick up and knit 28 (32, 40) sts around leg opening, dividing sts 3 needles. Place marker for beg of rnd and join.

Work 5 rnds of K2, P2 Rib.

Bind off in rib.

Rep for other leg opening.

FINISHING

Block to finished measurements.

Sew body seam from neckband to back edging.

Fold neckband in half and loosely tack edge to WS.

Weave in all ends. ∎

First-Class Wearables

You won't be able to resist these pullover and cardigan sweaters and stylish vests! Use any worsted weight yarn, but first read The Mystery of a Worsted Gauge, page 6.

Captivating Bolero

Self-striping or patterned yarn lends visual interest to a casual style with a modern fit and appeal.

Design by Jodi Snyder

SKILL LEVEL

■■■□ INTERMEDIATE

SIZES

Woman's small (medium, large, extra-large, 2X-large) Instructions are given for smallest size, with larger sizes in parentheses. When only 1 number is given, it applies to all sizes.

FINISHED MEASUREMENTS

Chest: 36 (40, 44, 48, 52) inches
Length: 19½ (20, 21½, 23, 23½) inches

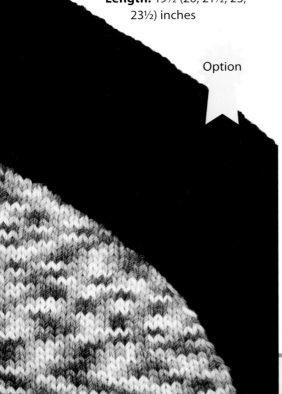

Option

MATERIALS

- **Featured yarn:** Plymouth Boku 95 percent wool/5 percent silk worsted weight yarn (99 yds/50g per ball): 4 (5, 6, 7, 8) balls blue/purple/green variegated #1 (MC) — **4** MEDIUM
- **Featured yarn:** Plymouth Cleckheaton Country 8 Ply 100 percent superwash wool light weight yarn (105 yds/50g per ball): 2 (3, 3, 3, 4) balls purple #2181 (CC) — **3** LIGHT
- **Option yarn:** Lily Chin Park Avenue Printed 60 percent merino wool/40 percent fine alpaca worsted weight yarn (109 yds/50g per ball): 4 (5, 6, 7, 8) balls gray/white variegated #101 (MC) — **4** MEDIUM
- **Option yarn:** Lily Chin Park Avenue 60 percent merino wool/40 percent fine alpaca worsted weight yarn (109 yds/50g per ball): 2 (3, 3, 3, 4) balls black #02 (CC)
- Size 6 (4.25mm) straight and 29-inch circular needles
- Size 7 (4.5mm) straight needles or size needed to obtain gauge
- Stitch markers
- Tapestry needle

GAUGE

16 sts and 24 rows = 4 inches/ 10cm in St st with larger needles
To save time, take time to check gauge.

SPECIAL ABBREVIATION

P1B (Purl 1 in row below): Insert RH needle from back-to-front into the st 1 row below next st on LH needle; purl this st, then purl the st on LH needle.

PATTERN STITCHES

A. K3, P3 Rib (multiple of 6 sts + 3)
Row 1 (WS): P3, *k3, p3; rep from * across.
Row 2: K3, *p3, k3; rep from * across.
Rep Rows 1 and 2 for pat.

B. K3, P3 Rib worked in the round (multiple of 6 sts)
Rnd 1: *K3, p3; rep from * around.
Rep Rnd 1 for pat.

PATTERN NOTES

Read instructions carefully before starting; several areas of shaping are worked *at the same time.*

Work incs and decs 1 st in from edge, unless stated otherwise.

BACK
With larger needles and MC, cast on 64 (72, 80, 88, 96) sts.

SHAPE WAIST
Beg with a WS row, work in St st, and *at the same time*, inc 1 st each side [every 10 rows] 4 (3, 0, 0, 0) times, then [every 12 rows] 0 (1, 4, 4, 4) times. (72, 80, 88, 96, 104 sts)

Work even until back measures 8 (8, 9, 10, 10) inches, ending with a WS row.

SHAPE ARMHOLES
Bind off 5 (6, 7, 8, 9) sts at beg of next 2 rows, then dec 1 st at each side [every RS row] 4 (6, 6, 7, 8) times. (54, 56, 62, 66, 70 sts)

Work even until armhole measures 8 (8½, 9, 9½, 10) inches, ending with a WS row.

SHAPE SHOULDERS
Bind off 15 (16, 18, 20, 20) sts at beg of next 2 rows.

Bind off rem 24 (24, 26, 26, 30) sts for neck.

LEFT FRONT
With larger needles and MC, cast on 8 (8, 12, 12, 16) sts.

Beg with a WS row, work 2 rows in St st.

SHAPE LOWER EDGE & WAIST
At front edge (beg of WS rows), cast on 3 sts [every WS row] 4 (4, 4, 5, 5) times and 2 sts [every WS row] 3 (5, 5, 5, 5) times, then inc 1 st at front edge [every WS row] 3 (3, 3, 4, 4) times, then [every 4 rows] twice; *at the same time*, at side edge (beg of RS rows), inc 1 st [every 10 rows] 4 (3, 0, 0, 0) times, then [every 12 rows] 0 (1, 4, 4, 4) times. (32, 36, 40, 44, 48 sts)

Work even in St st until piece measures 8 (8, 9, 10, 10) inches, ending with a WS row.

SHAPE ARMHOLE & NECK
Next row: Bind off 5 (6, 7, 8, 9) sts, work across. (27, 30, 33, 36, 39 sts)

Dec 1 st at armhole edge [every RS row] 4 (6, 6, 7, 8) times, and *at the same time,* dec 1 st at neck edge [every 6 rows] 5 (6, 6, 7, 5) times, then [every 4 rows] 3 (2, 3, 2, 6) times. (15, 16, 18, 20, 20 sts rem for shoulder)

Work even until armhole measures 8 (8½, 9, 9½, 10) inches, ending with a WS row.

Bind off rem sts.

RIGHT FRONT
With larger needles and MC, cast on 8 (8, 12, 12, 16) sts.

Beg with a WS row, work 1 row in St st.

SHAPE LOWER EDGE & WAIST
At front edge (beg of RS rows), cast on 3 sts [every RS row] 4 (4, 4, 5, 5) times and 2 sts [every RS row] 3 (5, 5, 5, 5) times, then inc 1 st at front edge [every RS row] 3 (3, 3, 4, 4) times, then [every 4 rows] 2 times; *at the same time*, at side edge (end of RS rows), inc 1 st [every 10 rows] 4 (3, 0, 0, 0) times, then [every 12 rows] 0 (1, 4, 4, 4) times. (32, 36, 40, 44, 48 sts)

Work even in St st until piece measures 8 (8, 9, 10, 10) inches, ending with a RS row.

SHAPE ARMHOLE & NECK
Bind off 5 (6, 7, 8, 9) sts, work across. (27, 30, 33, 36, 39 sts)

Dec 1 st at armhole edge [every RS row] 4 (6, 6, 7, 8) times; *at the same time*, dec 1 st at neck edge [every 6 rows] 5 (6, 6, 7, 5) times, then [every 4 rows] 3 (2, 3, 2, 6) times. (15, 16, 18, 20, 20 sts rem for shoulder)

Work even until armhole measures 8 (8½, 9, 9½, 10) inches, ending with a WS row.

Bind off rem sts.

SLEEVES
With smaller straight needles and CC, cast on 39 (39, 39, 45, 45) sts.

Work K3, P3 Rib for 3 inches, ending with a RS row.

Work 3 rows in rev St st.

Change to larger needle, MC and St st, and *at the same time*, inc 1 st each side [every 6 rows] 4 (5, 12, 6, 13) times, then [every 8 rows] 6 (6, 1, 6, 1) times. (59, 61, 65, 69, 73 sts)

Work even until sleeve measures 16½ (17½, 18, 18½, 19) inches from beg, ending with a WS row.

SHAPE CAP

Bind off 5 (6, 7, 8, 9) sts at beg of next 2 rows. (49, 49, 51, 53, 55 sts)

Dec 1 st each side [every other row] 9 (7, 8, 7, 8) times, [every 4 rows] 3 (5, 5, 6, 6) times. (25, 25, 25, 27, 27 sts)

Bind off 4 sts at beg of next 2 rows.

Bind off rem 17 (17, 17, 19, 19) sts.

FINISHING

Block pieces to finished measurements.

Sew shoulder seams. Set in sleeves. Sew sleeve and side seams.

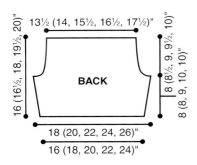

13½ (14, 15½, 16½, 17½)"
16 (16½, 18, 19½, 20)"
8 (8½, 9, 9½, 10)"
8 (8, 9, 10, 10)"
BACK
18 (20, 22, 24, 26)"
16 (18, 20, 22, 24)"
3¾ (4, 4½, 4, 4)"
3¾ (4, 4½, 4, 4)"
8 (8½, 9, 9½, 10)"
8 (8, 9, 10, 10)"
RIGHT FRONT
LEFT FRONT
8 (8½, 9, 9½, 10)"
8 (8, 9, 10, 10)"
8 (9, 10, 11, 12)"
8 (9, 10, 11, 12)"
14¾ (15¼, 16¼, 17¼, 18¼)"
16½ (17½, 18, 18½, 19)
SLEEVE
5½ (6, 6¼, 6¾, 7)"
13 (14, 14½, 15, 15½)"
3½"
9¾ (9¾, 9¾, 11¼, 11¼)"

BORDER

With RS facing and using CC and circular needle, beg at center back neck, pick up and knit 12 (12, 13, 13, 15) sts along back neck, 106 (111, 124, 132, 138) sts along left front, 64 (72, 80, 88, 96) across bottom of back, 106 (111, 124, 132, 138) sts along right front and 12 (12, 13, 13, 15) sts along back neck. (300, 318, 354, 378, 402 sts)

Join and place marker for beg of rnd.

Purl 3 rnds.

Work K3, P3 Rib until border measures 2 inches.

Next rnd: *K3, P1B, p2; rep from * around. (350, 371, 413, 441, 469 sts)

Continue in pat (working p4 instead of p3) until border measures 3½ inches.

Bind off loosely in pat. ■

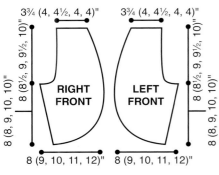

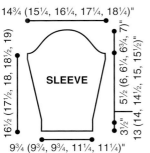

Tampa Vest

This vest is a wonderful knit for any climate. For warmer climes, it is lightweight and fun to wear. In colder weather, it adds a very fashionable layer!

Design by Julie Gaddy

SKILL LEVEL
■■■□ INTERMEDIATE

SIZES
Woman's small (medium, large, extra-large, 2X-large) Instructions are given for smallest size, with larger sizes in parentheses. When only 1 number is given, it applies to all sizes.

FINISHED MEASUREMENTS
Bust: 35 (40½, 43, 48½, 51) inches
Length: 20 (20, 20, 21, 22) inches

Option

MATERIALS
- **Featured yarn:** Lion Brand Cotton-Ease 50 percent cotton/50 percent acrylic worsted weight yarn (207 yds/100g per ball): 3 (3, 3, 4, 4) balls berry #112
- **Option yarn:** Plymouth Galway Worsted 100 percent wool worsted weight yarn (210 yds/100g per ball): 3 (3, 3, 4, 4) balls brown #152
- Size 5 (3.75mm) straight, 16-inch and 29-inch circular needles
- Size 8 (5mm) straight needles or size needed to obtain gauge
- Opening stitch markers or safety pins
- Tapestry needle

GAUGE
18 sts and 27 rows = 4 inches/10cm in pat st using larger needle
To save time, take time to check gauge.

PATTERN STITCH
Chevron Lace (multiple of 6 sts + 1)
Row 1 (RS): K1, *yo, ssk, k1, k2tog, yo, k1; rep from * across.
Rows 2 and 4: Purl.
Row 3: K1, *k1, yo, sk2p, yo, k2; rep from * across.
Rep Rows 1–4 for pat.

PATTERN NOTE
Specific instructions are given for shaping in lace.

BACK
Using smaller needles, cast on 79 (91, 97, 109, 115) sts.
Knit 4 rows.
Change to larger needles, and purl 1 row.
Beg with Row 1, work even in Chevron Lace until piece measures 10 (10, 10, 10, 11) inches from beg, ending with Row 4.

SHAPE ARMHOLES
Bind off 6 (6, 6, 12, 12) sts at beg of next 2 rows. (67, 79, 85, 85, 91 sts)
Work 2 rows even.
Dec in pat as follows:
Row 1: K1, ssk, k1, k2tog, yo, k1, *yo, ssk, k1, k2tog, yo, k1; rep from * to last 6 sts, yo, ssk, k1, k2tog, k1. (65, 77, 83, 83, 89 sts)
Row 2 and all WS rows: Purl.
Row 3: K1, ssk, k1, yo, k2, *k1, yo, sk2p, yo, k2; rep from * to last 5 sts, k1, yo, k1, k2tog, k1. (65, 77, 83, 83, 89 sts)
Row 5: K1, ssk, k2tog, yo, k1, *yo, ssk, k1, k2tog, yo, k1; rep from * to last 5 sts, yo, ssk, k2tog, k1. (63, 75, 81, 81, 87 sts)

Row 7: K1, ssk, k2, *k1, yo, sk2p, yo, k2; rep from * to last 4 sts, k1, k2tog, k1. (61, 73, 79, 79, 85 sts)

Row 9: K1, ssk, k1, *yo, ssk, k1, k2tog, yo, k1; rep from * to last 3 sts, k2tog, k1. (59, 71, 77, 77, 83 sts)

Row 11: K1, ssk, *k1, yo, sk2p, yo, k2; rep from * to last 8 sts, k1, yo, sk2p, yo, k1, k2tog, k1. (57, 69, 75, 75, 81 sts)

Row 12: Purl.

Working first and last sts in St st, work even in pat as established until piece measures approx 20 (20, 20, 21, 22) inches from beg, ending with Row 4 of pat.

Bind off knitwise.

RIGHT FRONT

Using smaller needles, cast on 38 (44, 50, 56, 56) sts.

Knit 4 rows.

Change to larger needles and purl 1 row.

Row 1 (RS): K1, work in Chevron Lace to end of row.

Maintaining front edge st in St st, work even in pat st until right front has 1 fewer pat rep than back before armhole bind off, or approx 9 (9, 9, 9, 10) inches, ending with Row 4.

SHAPE NECK & ARMHOLE

Row 1 (RS): K2tog, ssk, k1, k2tog, yo, k1, *yo, ssk, k1, k2tog, yo, k1; rep from * to end. (36, 42, 48, 54, 54 sts)

Row 2: Purl.

Row 3: K1, ssk, k1, yo, k2, *k1, yo, sk2p, yo, k2; rep from * to end. (36, 42, 48, 54, 54 sts)

Row 4: Bind off 6 (6, 12, 12, 12) sts, purl to end of row. (30, 36, 36, 42, 42 sts)

Row 5: K1, ssk, k2tog, yo, k1, *yo, ssk, k1, k2tog, yo, k1; rep from * to last 6 sts, yo, ssk, k1, k2tog, k1. (28, 34, 34, 40, 40 sts)

Row 6 and all rem WS rows: Purl.

Row 7: K1, ssk, k2, *k1, yo, sk2p, yo, k2; rep from * to last 5 sts, k1, yo, k1, k2tog, k1. (27, 33, 33, 39, 39 sts)

Row 9: K1, ssk, k1, *yo, ssk, k1, k2tog, yo, k1; rep from * to last 5 sts, yo, ssk, k2tog, k1. (25, 31, 31, 37, 37 sts)

Row 11: K1, ssk, *k1, yo, sk2p, yo, k2; rep from * to last 4 sts, k1, k2tog, k1. (23, 29, 29, 35, 35 sts)

Row 13: K1, ssk, k2, k2tog, yo, k1, *yo, ssk, k1, k2tog, yo, k1; rep from * to last 3 sts, k2tog, k1. (21, 27, 27, 33, 33 sts)

Row 15: K1, ssk, k2tog, yo, k2, *k1, yo, sk2p, yo, k2; rep from * to last 8 sts, k1, yo, sk2p, yo, k1, k2tog, k1. (19, 25, 25, 31, 31 sts)

SMALL, MEDIUM & LARGE SIZES ONLY

Row 17: K1, ssk, k2tog, yo, k1, *yo, ssk, k1, k2tog, yo, k1; rep from * to last st, k1. (18, 24, 24 sts)

Row 19: K1, ssk, k2, *k1, yo, sk2p, yo, k2; rep from * to last st, k1. (17, 23, 23 sts)

Row 21: K1, ssk, k1, *yo, ssk, k1, k2tog, yo, k1, rep from * to last st, k1. (16, 22, 22 sts)

Row 23: K1, ssk, *k1, yo, sk2p, yo, k2; rep from * to last st, k1. (15, 21, 21 sts)

EXTRA-LARGE & 2X-LARGE SIZES ONLY

Row 17: K1, ssk, k2tog, yo, k1, *yo, ssk, k1, k2tog, yo, k1; rep from * to last 7 sts, yo, ssk, k2, k2tog, k1. (29, 29 sts)

Row 19: K1, ssk, k2, *k1, yo, sk2p, yo, k2; rep from * to last 6 sts, k1, yo, ssk, k2tog, k1. (27, 27 sts)

Row 21: K1, ssk, k1, *yo, ssk, k1, k2tog, yo, k1; rep from * to last 5 sts, yo, ssk, k2tog, k1. (25, 25 sts)

Row 23: K1, ssk, *k1, yo, sk2p, yo, k2; rep from * to last 4 sts, k1, k2tog, k1. (23, 23 sts)

Row 25: K2, *yo, ssk, k1, k2tog, yo, k1; rep from * to last 3 sts, k2tog, k1. (22, 22 sts)

Row 27: K2, *k1, yo, sk2p, yo, k2; rep from * to last 8 sts, k1, yo, sk2p, yo, k1, k2tog, k1. (21, 21 sts)

ALL SIZES

Working first and last sts in St st, work even in pat as established until piece measures same as back, ending with Row 4.

Bind off knitwise.

LEFT FRONT

Using smaller needles, cast on 38 (44, 50, 56, 56) sts.

Knit 4 rows.

Change to larger needles and purl 1 row.

Row 1 (RS): Work in Chevron Lace to last st, k1.

Maintaining front edge st in St st, work even in pat st until left front measures same as right front to beg of neck, ending with Row 4.

SHAPE NECK & ARMHOLE

Row 1 (RS): K1, *yo, ssk, k1, k2tog, yo, k1; rep from * to last 7 sts, yo, ssk, k1, [k2tog] twice. (36, 42, 48, 54, 54 sts)

Row 2 and all WS rows: Purl

Row 3: K1, *k1, yo, sk2p, yo, k2; rep from * to last 5 sts, k1, yo, k1, k2tog, k1. (36, 42, 48, 54, 54 sts)

Row 5: Bind off 6 (6, 12, 12, 12) sts, work in pat as established to last 5 sts, yo, ssk, k2tog, k1. (29, 35, 35, 41, 41 sts)

Row 7: K1, ssk, k2, yo, k2, *k1, yo, sk2p, yo, k2; rep from * to last 4 sts, k1, k2tog, k1. (28, 34, 34, 40, 40 sts)

Row 9: K1, ssk, k1, k2tog, yo, k1, *yo, ssk, k1, k2tog, yo, k1; rep from * to last 3 sts, k2tog, k1. (26, 32, 32, 38, 38 sts)

Row 11: K1, ssk, k1, yo, k2, *k1, yo, sk2p, yo, k2; rep from * to last 8 sts, k1, yo, sk2p, yo, k1, k2tog, k1. (25, 31, 31, 37, 37 sts)

Row 13: K1, ssk, k2tog, yo, k1, *yo, ssk, k1, k2tog, yo, k1; rep from * to last 7 sts, yo, ssk, k2, k2tog, k1. (23, 29, 29, 35, 35 sts)

Row 15: K1, ssk, k2, *k1, yo, sk2p, yo, k2; rep from * to last 6 sts, k1, yo, ssk, k2tog, k1. (21, 27, 27, 33, 33 sts)

Row 17: K1, ssk, k1, *yo, ssk, k1, k2tog, yo, k1; rep from * to last 5 sts, yo, ssk, k2tog, k1. (19, 25, 25, 31, 31 sts)

Row 19: K1, ssk, *k1, yo, sk2p, yo, k2; rep from * to last 4 sts, k1, k2tog, k1. (17, 23, 23, 29, 29 sts)

SMALL, MEDIUM & LARGE SIZES ONLY

Row 21: K2, *yo, ssk, k1, k2tog, yo, k1; rep from * to last 3 sts, k2tog, k1. (16, 22, 22 sts)

Row 23: K2, *k1, yo, sk2p, yo, k2; rep from * to last 8 sts, k1, yo, sk2p, yo, k1, k2tog, k1. (15, 21, 21 sts)

EXTRA-LARGE & 2X-LARGE SIZES ONLY

Row 21: K1, ssk, k2, k2tog, yo, k1, *yo, ssk, k1, k2tog, yo, k1; rep from * to last 3 sts, k2tog, k1. (27, 27 sts)

Row 23: K1, ssk, k2tog, yo, k2, *k1, yo, sk2p, yo, k2; rep from * to last 8 sts, k1, yo, sk2p, yo, k1, k2tog, k1. (25, 25 sts)

Row 25: K1, ssk, k2tog, yo, k1, *k1, yo, ssk, k1, k2tog, yo, k1; rep from * to last st, k1. (24, 24 sts)

Row 27: K1, ssk, k3, *yo, sk2p, yo, k3; rep from * to end. (23, 23 sts)

Row 29: K1, ssk, k1, *yo, ssk, k1, k2tog, yo, k1; rep from * to last st, k1. (22, 22 sts)

Row 31: K1, ssk, *k1, yo, sk2p, yo, k2; rep from * to last st, k1. (21, 21 sts)

ALL SIZES

Working first and last sts in St st, work even in pat as established until piece measures approx 20 (20, 20, 21, 22) inches from beg, ending with Row 4 of pat.

Bind off knitwise.

FINISHING

Block all pieces to finished measurements.

Sew shoulder seams and side seams.

ARMHOLE BANDS

With RS facing and using shorter circular needle, beg at underarm seam, pick up and knit 120 (120, 120, 125, 130) sts around armhole, place marker and join.

Purl 1 rnd, knit 1 rnd, purl 1 rnd, knit 1 rnd.

Bind off purlwise.

FRONT BAND

Mark first dec row of V-neck on each front with opening markers or safety pins.

With RS facing and using longer circular needle, beg at lower edge of right front, pick up and knit 55 (55, 55, 55, 60) sts to first marker, 55 (55, 55, 60, 60) sts to right shoulder seam, 27 (27, 33, 33, 37)

sts across back neck, 55 (55, 55, 60, 60) sts from left shoulder seam to 2nd marker, 2nd 55 (55, 55, 55, 60) sts to bottom edge of left front. Do not join.

Knit 4 rows.

Bind off knitwise.

Weave in all ends. ■

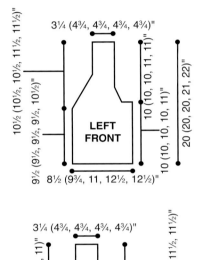

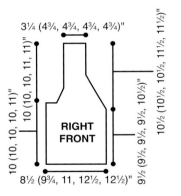

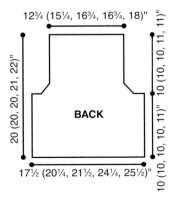

Chic & Cabled Top

This is the perfect cabled pullover for first-time "cablers." These wavelike cables will create a sweater that is just right for the beach.

Design by Kathy Sasser

Feature

SKILL LEVEL

 EASY

SIZES

Woman's small (medium, large, extra-large, 2X-large) Instructions are given for smallest size, with larger sizes in parentheses. When only 1 number is given, it applies to all sizes.

FINISHED MEASUREMENTS

Chest: 36 (40, 44, 48, 52) inches
Length: 22 (22½, 23, 23½, 24) inches

MATERIALS

- **Featured yarn:** S.R. Kertzer Super 10 Worsted 100 percent cotton worsted weight yarn (249 yds/125g per skein): 4 (5, 6, 7, 7) skeins Capri green #3765
- **Option yarn:** TLC Essentials 100 percent acrylic worsted weight yarn (312 yds/170g per skein): 3 (4, 4, 5, 5) skeins Eden green #2680
- Size 6 (4mm) 24-inch circular needle
- Size 7 (4.5mm) 24-inch circular needles or size needed to obtain gauge
- Stitch markers
- Cable needle
- Safety pins
- Stitch holders
- Tapestry needle

GAUGE

20 sts and 26 rows = 4 inches/10cm in St st on larger needle
   To save time, take time to check gauge.

SPECIAL ABBREVIATIONS

C6B (Cable 6 Back): Sl next 3 sts to cn and hold in back; k3, then k3 from cn.
C6F (Cable 6 Front): Sl next 3 sts to cn and hold in front; k3, then k3 from cn.

SPECIAL TECHNIQUE
3-Needle Bind Off

With RS tog and needles parallel, using a 3rd needle, knit tog a st from the front needle with 1 from the back. *Knit tog a st from the front and back needles, and sl the first st over the 2nd to bind off. Rep from * across, then fasten off last st.

PATTERN STITCH
Wavy Cable (6-st panel)

Rnds 1–7: K6.
Rnd 8: C6B.
Rnds 9–15: K6.
Rnd 16: C6F.
Rep Rnds 1–16 for pat.

PATTERN NOTES

Sweater is worked in the round to armholes, then divided and worked back and forth; the sleeves are worked back and forth.

   When working in rows, keep cable panel in established pat by knitting the knit sts and purling the purl sts as they face you on both sides and working cables on correct RS rows.

BODY

With smaller needle, cast on 180 (200, 220, 240, 260) sts; place marker for beg of rnd and join, being careful not to twist sts.
Set-up rnd: K90 (100, 110, 120, 130) for front, place marker for right side seam line, k90 (100, 110, 120, 130) sts for back.

   Knit 5 rnds, marking last rnd with a safety pin at center front.
Next rnd: Change to larger needle and knit.
Next rnd (Cable 1 setup): K6 (7, 9, 11, 13), place marker, inc 3 sts evenly across next 18 sts to form 21-st cable panel, place marker, knit to end of rnd. (183, 203, 223, 243, 263 sts)
Rnds 1–32: Knit to first marker, sl marker, p3, work Wavy Cable pat, p3, k9, sl marker, knit to end of rnd.

Option

Next rnd (Cable 2 setup): Knit to first marker, sl marker, *p3, work Wavy Cable pat; rep from * once, p3, sl marker, knit to end of rnd.

Continue in pats as established until piece measures 13½ (14, 14, 14, 14½) inches from safety pin, ending on any odd-numbered rnd.

LEFT FRONT & NECK SHAPING

Next row (RS): Work 40 (44, 48, 53, 57) sts in pat, sl rem sts to smaller circular needle for holder; turn.

Dec row (WS): P1, p2tog, work to end of row. (39, 43, 47, 52, 56 sts)

Continue in pats as established and rep Dec row [every other row] 7 (8, 9, 9, 10) times. (32, 35, 38, 43, 46 sts)

Work even until left front measures 8½ (8½, 9, 9½, 9½) inches from beg of armhole, ending with a RS row.

Next row (WS): Removing markers, purl to 1 st before marker, [k2tog, k1, p6] 3 times, purl to end of row. (29, 32, 35, 40, 43 sts)

Place sts on a holder.

RIGHT FRONT

Place 16 (18, 20, 20, 22) center front sts on a st holder.

Attach yarn to next st on LH needle and with larger needle, knit to side marker, turn. (37, 41, 45, 50, 54 sts)

Dec row (WS): Purl to last 3 sts, ssp, p1. (36, 40, 44, 49, 53 sts)

Continue in St st and rep Dec row [every other row] 7 (8, 9, 9, 10) times. (29, 32, 35, 40, 43 sts)

Work even until right front measures same as left front to shoulder.

Place sts on a holder.

BACK

With RS facing, attach yarn to back at right side edge.

With larger needle, work in St st until back measures same as front to shoulder.

Place sts on holder or spare needle.

LEFT SLEEVE

**With smaller needle, cast on 44 (48, 48, 50, 52) sts; do not join.

Beg with a RS row, work in St st for 6 rows.

Place a safety pin at beg and end of last row.

Change to larger needle.**

Inc 1 st each end [every 4 (5, 4, 4, 4) rows] 8 (18, 6, 12, 3) times, then [every 5 (6, 5, 5, 5) rows] 14 (2, 16, 12, 20) times. (88, 88, 92, 98, 98 sts)

Work even until sleeve measures 16½ (16½, 17, 17½, 18) inches from safety pins.

Bind off.

RIGHT SLEEVE

Work as for left sleeve from ** to **.

Work inc as for left sleeve and *at the same time* work center cable panel as follows:

Set-up row (RS): K17 (19, 19, 20, 21), place marker, inc 2 sts evenly across next 10 sts to form 12-st cable panel, place marker, k17 (19, 19, 20, 21) sts. (46, 50, 50, 52, 54 sts)

Rows 1, 3, 5, 7 (WS): Purl to marker, sl marker, k3, p6, k3, sl marker, purl to end.

Rows 2, 4, 6 (RS): Knit to marker, sl marker, p3, k6, p3, sl marker, knit to end.

Row 8: Knit to marker, sl marker, p3, C6B, p3, sl marker, knit to end.

Rows 9, 11, 13 and 15: Rep Row 1.

Rows 10, 12 and 14: Rep Row 2.

Row 16: Knit to marker, sl marker, p3, C6F, p3, sl marker, knit to end.

Continue in pat as established until right sleeve measures same as left sleeve.

Bind off.

FINISHING

Block pieces to finished measurements.

Bind off shoulders tog using 3-needle bind off, leaving center back 32 (36, 40, 40, 44) sts on needle.

COLLAR

With RS facing and smaller needle, beg at left shoulder, pick up and knit 44 (44, 47, 49, 49) sts along left neck edge, knit center front 16 (18, 20, 20, 22) sts, pick up and knit 44 (44, 47, 49, 49) sts along right neck edge, then knit across center back 32 (36, 40, 40, 44) sts, place marker for beg of rnd and join. (136, 142, 154, 158, 164 sts)

Knit 6 rnds.

Bind off.

SEW ON SLEEVES

With WS facing and using mattress st, sew sleeve seam from cast-on edge to markers.

With RS facing and using mattress st, sew sleeve seams from markers to top.

Weave in all ends. ∎

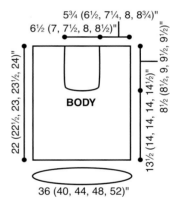

5¾ (6½, 7¼, 8, 8¾)"
6½ (7, 7½, 8, 8½)"
8½ (8½, 9, 9½, 9½)"
22 (22½, 23, 23½, 24)"
13½ (14, 14, 14, 14½)"
BODY
36 (40, 44, 48, 52)"

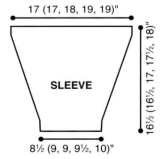

17 (17, 18, 19, 19)"
SLEEVE
16½ (16½, 17, 17½, 18)"
8½ (9, 9, 9½, 10)"

Traveler's Jacket

When you want to pack something to wear over anything, from a dinner dress to jeans, this is the sweater to rely on for a stunning look.

Design by Debbie O'Neill

SKILL LEVEL
■■■□□ EASY

SIZES
Women's extra-small (small, medium, large, extra-large, 2X-large) Instructions are given for smallest size, with larger sizes in parentheses. When only 1 number is given, it applies to all sizes.

FINISHED MEASUREMENTS
Chest: 34 (37, 40, 44, 47, 50) inches
Length: 21 (22, 23, 24, 25, 26) inches

Option

MATERIALS
- **Featured yarn:** Knit One, Crochet Too Paint Box 100 percent wool worsted weight yarn (100 yds/50g per ball): 8 (9, 10, 11, 12, 14) balls gold rush #17

  4 MEDIUM

- **Option yarn:** Moda Dea Eclipse 60 percent extra-fine wool/40 percent nylon worsted weight yarn (125 yds/50g per ball): 7 (8, 8, 9, 10, 12) balls mauve #2561
- Size 7 (4.5mm) knitting needles or size needed to obtain gauge
- Size G/6 (4mm) crochet hook
- Stitch holders
- Tapestry needle
- 1 button, at least 1-inch in diameter

GAUGE
20 sts and 28 rows = 4 inches/10cm in Rice St
  To save time, take time to check gauge.

SPECIAL TECHNIQUE
3-Needle Bind Off
With RS tog and needles parallel, using a 3rd needle, knit a st from the front needle and 1 from the back tog. *Knit a st from the front and back needles tog, and sl the first st over the 2nd to bind off. Rep from * across, then fasten off last st.

PATTERN STITCH
Rice St (multiple of 2 sts + 1)
Row 1 (WS): Knit.
Row 2: P1, *k1-tbl, p1; rep from * across.
  Rep Rows 1 and 2 for pat.

BACK
Cast on 85 (93, 101, 111, 117, 125) sts.
  Work even in Rice St until piece measures 13 (13½, 14, 14½, 15, 15½) inches or desired length to armhole, ending with a WS row.

SHAPE ARMHOLE
Bind off 4 (5, 5, 7, 7, 9) sts at beg of next 2 rows. (77, 83, 91, 97, 103, 107 sts)
  Dec 1 st each side [every row] 4 (4, 6, 6, 8, 8) times. (69, 75, 79, 85, 87, 91 sts)
  Work even until armhole measures 8 (8½, 9, 9½, 10, 10½) inches, ending with a RS row.
Next row (WS): K20 (22, 23, 24, 24, 25), bind off 29 (31, 33, 37, 39, 41) sts, k20 (22, 23, 24, 24, 25).
  Place rem sts on holders for shoulders.

LEFT FRONT

Cast on 43 (47, 51, 57, 59, 63) sts.

Work even in Rice St until piece measures 13 (13½, 14, 14½, 15, 15½) inches or desired length to armhole, ending with a WS row.

SHAPE ARMHOLE

Next row (RS): Bind off 4 (5, 5, 7, 7, 9) sts, work in pat to end. (39, 42, 46, 50, 52, 54 sts)

Dec 1 st at armhole edge [every row] 4 (4, 6, 6, 8, 8) times. (35, 38, 40, 44, 44, 46 sts)

Work even until armhole measures 2 (2½, 3, 2½, 3, 3½) inches, ending with a RS row.

SHAPE NECK

Dec row (WS): K1, ssk, knit to end of row. (34, 37, 39, 43, 43, 45 sts)

Continue in pat and rep Dec row [every other row] 14 (15, 16, 19, 19, 20) times. (20, 22, 23, 24, 24, 25 sts)

Work even until piece measures 21 (22, 23, 24, 25, 26) inches, ending with a RS row.

Sl rem sts to holder.

RIGHT FRONT

Cast on 43 (47, 51, 57, 59, 63) sts.

Work even in Rice St until piece measures 13 (13½, 14, 14½, 15, 15½) inches or desired length to armhole, ending with a RS row.

SHAPE ARMHOLE

Next row (WS): Bind off 4 (5, 5, 7, 7, 9) sts, work in pat to end. (39, 42, 46, 50, 52, 54 sts)

Dec 1 st at armhole edge [every row] 4 (4, 6, 6, 8, 8) times. (35, 38, 40, 44, 44, 46 sts) Work even in pat until armhole measures 2 (2½, 3, 2½, 3, 3½) inches, ending with a RS row.

SHAPE NECK

Dec row (WS): Knit to last 3 sts, k2tog, k1. (34, 37, 39, 43, 43, 45 sts)

Continue in pat and rep Dec row [every other row] 14 (15, 16, 19, 19, 20) times. (20, 22, 23, 24, 24, 25 sts)

Work even in pat until piece measures 21 (22, 23, 24, 25, 26) inches.

Sl rem sts to holder.

SLEEVES

Cast on 53 (57, 61, 65, 69, 73) sts.

Work Rice St and inc 1 st at each end [every 4 rows] 14 (14,

15, 15, 16, 16) times. (81, 85, 91, 95, 101, 105 sts)

Work even until piece measures 13 (13½, 14, 14½, 15, 15) inches.

Dec 1 each side [every row] 4 (4, 6, 6, 8, 8) times. (73, 77, 79, 83, 85, 89 sts)

Bind off all sts.

FINISHING

Block all pieces to finished measurements.

Join shoulder seams using 3-needle bind off.

Sew in sleeves, working from shoulder to armhole.

Sew side and underarm seams.

FRONT & NECK EDGING

Row 1: With RS facing and using crochet hook, beg at lower edge of front opening, work 1 row sc to opposite lower edge of front opening; do not turn.

Row 2: With RS still facing, work sc in opposite direction (left to right if right-handed, right to left if left-handed).

Sew button to the base of the V-neck on right front.

Crochet a short chain and attach both ends at the base of the V-neck on left front opposite button.

Weave in all ends. ■

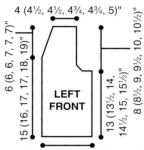

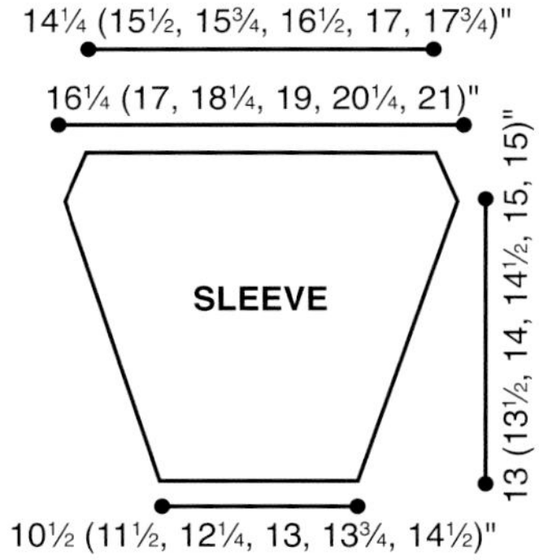

4 (4½, 4½, 4¾, 4¾, 5)"

6 (6, 6, 7, 7, 7)"

LEFT FRONT

15 (16, 17, 17, 18, 19)"

8 (8½, 9, 9½, 10, 10½)"

13 (13½, 14, 14½, 15, 15½)"

8½ (9½, 10¼, 11½, 11¾, 12½)"

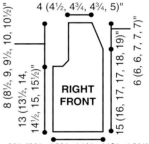

4 (4½, 4¾, 4¾, 5)"

8 (8½, 9, 9½, 10, 10½)"

RIGHT FRONT

6 (6, 6, 7, 7, 7)"

15 (16, 17, 17, 18, 19)"

13 (13½, 14, 14½, 15, 15½)"

8½ (9½, 10¼, 11½, 11¾, 12½)"

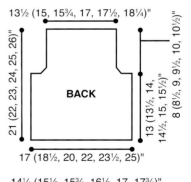

13½ (15, 15¾, 17, 17½, 18¼)"

21 (22, 23, 24, 25, 26)"

BACK

8 (8½, 9, 9½, 10, 10½)"

13 (13½, 14, 14½, 15, 15½)"

17 (18½, 20, 22, 23½, 25)"

14¼ (15½, 15¾, 16½, 17, 17¾)"

16¼ (17, 18¼, 19, 20¼, 21)"

SLEEVE

13 (13½, 14, 14½, 15, 15)"

10½ (11½, 12¼, 13, 13¾, 14½)"

Peace of Mind Hoodie

Choose a natural cotton or linen yarn and create a sweater that is oh so relaxed. You'll love its modern-classic styling.

Design by Scarlet Taylor

SKILL LEVEL

■■■□ INTERMEDIATE

SIZES

Woman's small (medium, large, extra-large, 2X-large) Instructions are given for smallest size, with larger sizes in parentheses. When only 1 number is given, it applies to all sizes.

FINISHED MEASUREMENTS

Chest: 39 (42, 45, 48, 51) inches
Length: 24½ (25½, 25½, 26½, 26½) inches

Option

MATERIALS

- **Featured yarn:** J.&P. Coats Royale Quick Crochet 75 percent cotton/25 percent acrylic worsted weight thread (400 yds per ball): 4 (5, 5, 6, 6) balls linen marl #1008
- **Option yarn:** Moda Dea Fashionista 50 percent acrylic/50 percent Tencel/ Lyocell worsted weight yarn (183 yds/100g per ball): 9 (11, 11, 13, 13) balls boysenberry #6131
- Size 7 (4.5mm) circular needle
- Size 8 (5mm) knitting needles
- Size 9 (5.5mm) knitting needles, or size needed to obtain gauge
- Stitch holders
- Tapestry needle

GAUGE

16 sts and 26 rows = 4 inches/10cm in pat st
   To save time, take time to check your gauge.

PATTERN STITCH

Open Star St (multiple of 3 sts + 5)
Row 1 (WS): P1 (edge st), k2, *yo, k3; insert left-needle from left to right into the first of these 3 knitted sts, lift it over the other 2 sts and off the right-hand needle as in psso; rep from * to last 2 sts, k1, p1 (selvage st).
Row 2: Knit across row, including all yo's.
Row 3: P1 (edge st), k1, *k3, lift first of these 3 sts over the other 2 as before, yo; rep from * to last 3 sts, k2, p1 (edge st).
Row 4: Rep Row 2.
   Rep Rows 1–4 for pat.

PATTERN NOTES

St count includes 2 edge sts for seaming. They are not included in total measurements.
   A circular needle is used for ribbing in order to accommodate large number of sts for edging around neck and hood.

BACK

With size 7, cast on 80 (86, 92, 98, 104) sts.
   Work in K1, P1 Rib until piece measures approx 1 inches, ending with a RS row.
   Change to size 9 needles, and work Open Star St until piece measures approx 15½ (16, 15½, 16, 15½) inches from beg, ending with a WS row.

SHAPE ARMHOLES

Bind off 8 (8, 8, 9, 9) sts at beg of next 2 rows. (64, 70, 76, 80, 86 sts)

Work even until armhole measures 8 (8½, 9, 9½, 10) inches from beg, ending with a WS row.

SHAPE SHOULDERS

Bind off 5 (6, 7, 8, 9) sts at beg of next 4 rows, then bind off 6 (7, 8, 8, 9) sts at beg of next 2 rows.

Sl center 32 sts onto st holder for back neck.

FRONT

Work same as for Back until piece measures approx 14½ (15½, 14½, 15½, 14½) inches from beg, ending with a WS row.

SHAPE NECK & ARMHOLES

Next row (RS): Work across first 37 (40, 43, 46, 49) sts in pat as established, k2tog, k1; join a 2nd ball of yarn, k1, ssk, work in pat to end of row.

Work both sides at once with separate balls of yarn, and maintaining neck edge st and dec st in St st throughout, work 3 rows even; *at the same time*, when piece measures same as back to armhole, bind off armholes as for back.

Dec row (RS): Work in pat as established to last 3 sts, k2tog, k1; k1, ssk, work in pat to end of row.

Rep Dec row every 4 (4, 6, 6, 6) rows 1 (1, 6, 6, 4) time(s), then every 6 (6, 8, 8, 8) rows 7 (7, 2, 2, 4) times. (22, 25, 28, 30, 33 sts each side)

Bind off 2 sts at each neck edge twice for hood neck edge. (18, 21, 24, 26, 29 sts each side)

Rep Dec row on following 2 RS rows. (16, 19, 22, 24, 27 sts each side)

Work even until piece measures same as back to shoulder edge, ending with a WS row.

SHAPE SHOULDERS

Work same as for back.

SLEEVES

With size 7 needles, cast on 35 (35, 38, 38, 44) sts.

Work in K1, P1 rib until piece measures approx 1 inch, ending with a RS row.

Next row (WS): Change to size 9 needles work Row 1 of Open Star St pat.

Inc row (RS): K1, M1, knit to last st, M1, k1.

Continue in pat and rep Inc row [every 6 rows] 4 (11, 11, 18, 17) times, then [every 8 rows] 10 (5, 5, 0, 0) times, working extra sts into pat as they become available. (65, 69, 72, 76, 80 sts)

Work even until piece measures 20¾ (21, 21¼, 21½, 21½) inches from beg, ending with a WS row.

Bind off.

FINISHING

Block all pieces to finished measurements.

Sew shoulder seams.

HOOD

With size 8 needles, beg at hood neck edge, pick up and knit 54 sts evenly around neck edge, ending at opposite hood neck edge.

Work even in St st for 1 inch, ending with a WS row.

Next row (RS): K5, M1, [k4, M1] 11 times, k5. (66 sts)

Work 9 rows even in St st.

Next row (RS): K5, M1, [k7, M1] 8 times, k5. (75 sts)

Work 9 rows even.

Next row (RS): K6, M1, [k8, M1] 8 times, k5. (84 sts)

Work even until hood measures approx 14 inches, ending with a WS row.

Bind off.

Fold bind-off edge in half, and sew top hood seam.

HOOD & V-NECK BORDER

With size 7 circular needle, beg at base of V-neck shaping, pick up and knit 194 sts evenly around neck shaping and hood, ending at opposite base of V-neck; do not join.

Work back and forth in K1, P1 Rib for 1 inch, ending with a WS row.

Bind off loosely in rib.

Overlap border at base and st in place.

Set in sleeves. Sew sleeve and side seams.

Weave in all ends.

Re-block as necessary. ■

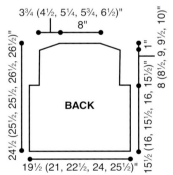

3¾ (4½, 5¼, 5¾, 6½)"
8"

24½ (25½, 25½, 26½, 26½)"

BACK

1"

8 (8½, 9, 9½, 10)"

15½ (16, 15½, 16, 15½)"

19½ (21, 22½, 24, 25½)"

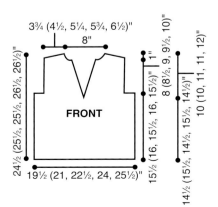

3¾ (4½, 5¼, 5¾, 6½)"
8"

24½ (25½, 25½, 26½, 26½)"

FRONT

1"

8 (8½, 9, 9½, 10)"

15½ (16, 15½, 16, 15½)"

10 (10, 11, 11, 12)"

14½ (15½, 14½, 15½, 14½)"

19½ (21, 22½, 24, 25½)"

16 (17, 18, 19, 20)"

SLEEVE

20¾ (21, 21¼, 21½, 21½)"

8¼ (8¼, 9, 9, 10½)"

Play Misty

Shaded yarn of any fiber is perfect for this scoop-necked, comfortably fitting pullover with easy-knit rolled edges.

Design by Kathy Perry

SKILL LEVEL
■■□□ EASY

SIZES
Women's small (medium, large, extra-large, 2X-large) Instructions are given for smallest size, with larger sizes in parentheses. When only 1 number is given, it applies to all sizes.

Option

FINISHED MEASUREMENTS
Chest: 38 (42, 46, 50, 54) inches
Length: 27 (27½, 28, 28½, 29) inches

MATERIALS
- **Featured yarn:** Caron International Simply Soft Shadows 100 percent acrylic worsted weight yarn (150 yds/3 oz per skein): 7 (7, 8, 8, 9) skeins plum mist #0002*
- **Option yarn:** Patons SWS 70 percent wool/30 percent soy worsted weight yarn (110 yds/80g per ball): 10 (10, 11, 11, 13) balls new denim #70117
- Size 8 (5mm) straight and 16-inch circular needles or size needed to obtain gauge
- Stitch holders
- Tapestry needle

*Yarn is self-striping. Stripe matching is not necessary, but if stripe matching is desired, extra yarn is required.

GAUGE
17 sts and 23 rows = 4 inches/10cm in St st
To save time, take time to check gauge.

PATTERN STITCH
K2, P2 Rib (multiple of 4 sts +2)
Row 1 (RS): K2, *p2, k2; rep from * across.
Row 2: P2, *k2, p2; rep from * across.
Rep Rows 1 and 2 for pat.

PATTERN NOTE
St count includes 2 edge sts for seaming. They are not included in total measurements.

BACK
Cast on 84 (91, 100, 108, 117) sts.
Work even in St st until piece measures 18 inches from beg, ending with a WS row.

SHAPE ARMHOLES
Bind off 5 (5, 6, 6, 7) sts at beg of next 2 rows. (74, 81, 88, 96, 103 sts)
Work even until armhole measures 9 (9½, 10, 10½, 11) inches, ending with a WS row.

SHOULDERS
Bind off 18 (22, 25, 28, 32) sts at beg of next 2 rows.
Place rem 38 (37, 38, 40, 39) sts on holder for back neck.

FRONT

Work as for back until armhole measures 3½ (4, 4½, 4½, 5) inches, ending with a WS row.

SHAPE NECK & SHOULDERS

Next row (RS): Work 28 (31, 35, 38, 41) sts, sl 18 (19, 18, 20, 21) sts to a holder, with a 2nd ball of yarn, work rem 28 (31, 35, 41) sts.

Working both sides *at the same time,* dec 1 at neck edge [every row] 5 (4, 5, 5, 4) times, then [every other row] 5 times. (18, 22, 25, 28, 32 sts)

Work even until armhole measures same as back.

Bind off shoulder sts.

SLEEVES

Cast on 42 (42, 42, 42, 46) sts.

Work in St st for 6 rows.

Work in K2, P2 Rib for 4 rows.

Working the rest of sleeve in St st, inc 1 st each edge [every 4 (4, 3, 3, 3) rows] 2 (17, 1, 3, 8) time(s), then [every 5 (5, 4, 4, 4) rows] 16 (4, 21, 21, 17) times. (78, 84, 86, 91, 96 sts)

Work even until sleeve measures 18½ (18½, 18½, 19½,

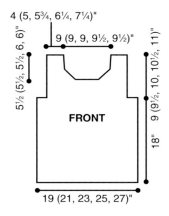

4 (5, 5¾, 6¼, 7¼)"

9 (9, 9, 9½, 9½)"

5½ (5½, 5½, 6, 6)"

9 (9½, 10, 10½, 11)"

FRONT

18"

19 (21, 23, 25, 27)"

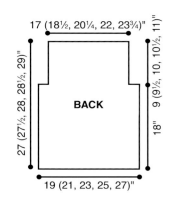

17 (18½, 20¼, 22, 23¾)"

9 (9½, 10, 10½, 11)"

27 (27½, 28, 28½, 29)"

BACK

18"

19 (21, 23, 25, 27)"

18 (19, 20, 21, 22)"

17 (17, 17, 18, 18)"

18½ (18½, 18½, 19½, 19½)"

SLEEVE

1½"

9½ (9½, 9½, 9½, 10½)"

19½) inches from beg.
  Bind off all sts.

ASSEMBLY

Block all pieces to finished measurements.
  Sew shoulder seams.

NECK EDGING

With RS facing and using circular needle, k38 (37, 38, 40, 39) sts from back neck holder, pick up and knit 27 (27, 27, 29, 29) sts from left front neck edge, k18 (19, 18, 20, 21) sts from right front neck holder, pick up and knit 27 (27, 27, 29, 29) sts from right front neck edge; place marker and join. (110, 110, 110, 118, 118 sts)
  Knit 9 rnds.
  Work 4 rnds in K2, P2 Rib.
  Knit 6 rnds.
  Bind off all sts loosely.

FINISHING

Sew in sleeves.
  Sew side and underarm seams, letting bottom edge and cuffs roll naturally.
  Let neck edging roll naturally and tack in place.
  Weave in all ends. ∎

City Girl Cardigan

Choose black and white for timeless drama, or combine two of your favorite wardrobe shades for a simple shape with visual interest.

Design by Melissa Leapman

SKILL LEVEL
■■■□ INTERMEDIATE

SIZES
Woman's small (medium, large, extra-large, 2X-large) Instructions are given for smallest size, with larger sizes in parentheses. When only 1 number is given, it applies to all sizes.

FINISHED MEASUREMENTS
Chest: 33½ (39, 40½, 46, 48) inches
Length: 24 (24½, 25, 25½, 25½) inches

MATERIALS
- **Featured yarn:** N.Y. Yarns Olympic 30 percent wool/70 percent acrylic worsted weight yarn (130 yds/50g per ball): 5 (6, 7, 8, 9) balls black #11 (A) and 4 (5, 6, 7, 8) balls cream #01 (B)
- **Option yarn:** TLC Cotton Plus 51 percent cotton/49 percent acrylic worsted weight yarn (178 yds/100g per skein): 4 (5, 6, 6, 7) skeins tan #3303 (A) and 3 (4, 5, 6, 6) skeins spruce #3503 (B)
- Size 9 (5.5mm) needles or size needed to obtain gauge
- Tapestry needle

▣ 4 MEDIUM

GAUGE
18 sts and 32 rows = 4 inches/10cm in pat
    To save time, take time to check gauge.

PATTERN NOTE
Sl sts purlwise with yarn to WS.

PATTERN STITCH
Mosaic Pat (multiple of 8 sts + 5)
Rows 1 (RS) and 2: With A, knit.
Row 3: With B, k1, *sl 1, k1, sl 1, k5; rep from * to last 4 sts, [sl 1, k1] twice.

Row 4: With B, k1, *sl 1, p1, sl 1, k5; rep from * to last 4 sts, sl 1, p1, sl 1, k1.
Row 5: With A, k2, *sl 1, k7; rep from * to last 3 sts, sl 1, k2.
Row 6: With A, k1, *p1, sl 1, p1, k5; rep from * to last 4 sts, p1, sl 1, p1, k1.
Rows 7–10: Rep Rows 3–6.
Row 11: With B, k5, *sl 1, k1, sl 1, k5; rep from * across.
Row 12: With B, k5, *sl 1, p1, sl 1, k5; rep from * across.
Row 13: With A, k6, *sl 1, k7; rep from * to last 7 sts, sl 1, k6.
Row 14: With A, k5, *p1, sl 1, p1, k5; rep from * across.
Rows 15–18: Rep Rows 11–14.
    Rep Rows 3–18 only for pat.

BACK
With A, cast on 77 (85, 93, 101, 109) sts.
    Work Sl St pat for 3 inches, ending with a WS row.

SHAPE WAIST
Dec 1 st each side on next row, and then [every 16 rows] twice. (71, 79, 87, 95, 103 sts)
    Work even until piece measures 9½ (9¾, 9¾, 9¾, 9¾) inches from beg, ending with a WS row.

Option

Inc 1 st each side on next row, and then [every 12 rows] twice. (77, 85, 93, 101, 109 sts)

Work even until piece measures 15 inches, ending with a WS row.

SHAPE ARMHOLES

Bind off 4 (6, 8, 8, 10) sts at beg of next 2 rows, then 2 (2, 2, 3, 3) sts at beg of following 2 rows.

Dec 1 st each side [every row] 1 (3, 4, 6, 8) time(s), then [every other row] 4 (3, 3, 3, 2) times. (55, 57, 59, 61, 63 sts)

Work even until piece measures 22½ (23, 23½, 24, 24) inches from beg, ending with a WS row.

SHAPE NECK

Work 14 (15, 16, 17, 18) sts, join 2nd ball of yarn and bind off middle 27 sts, work to end of row.

Working both sides at once with separate balls of yarn, dec 1 st each neck edge once. (13, 14, 15, 16, 17 sts each side)

Work even until piece measures approx 23 (23½, 24, 24½, 24½) inches from beg.

SHAPE SHOULDERS

Bind off 3 (4, 4, 4, 4) sts at beg of next 6 rows, then 4 (2, 3, 4, 5) sts at beg of following 2 rows.

LEFT FRONT

With A, cast on 37 (45, 45, 53, 53) sts.

Work even in Mosaic pat for 3 inches, ending with a WS row.

SHAPE WAIST

Dec 1 st at beg of next row, and then [every 16 rows] twice. (34, 42, 42, 50, 50 sts)

Work even until piece measures approx 9½ (9¾, 9¾, 9¾, 9¾) inches from beg, ending with a WS row.

Inc 1 st at beg of next row and then [every 12 rows] twice. (37, 45, 45, 53, 53 sts)

At the same time, when piece measures approx 11 (11½, 12, 12½, 12½) inches, ending with a RS row, shape neck as follows:

SHAPE NECK & ARMHOLE

Dec 1 st at beg of next row, then dec 1 st at neck edge [every 6 rows] 3 times, [every 8 rows] 9 times, and *at the same time*, when piece measures approx 15 inches from beg, bind off 4 (6, 8, 8, 10) sts at armhole edge once, then bind off 2 (2, 2, 3, 3) sts at armhole edge once, then dec 1 st at armhole edge [every row] 1 (3, 4, 6, 8) times, then [every other row] 4 (3, 3, 3, 2) times. (13, 14, 15, 16, 17 sts rem)

Work even in pat as established until piece measures same as back to shoulder, ending with a WS row.

SHAPE SHOULDER

Bind off 3 (4, 4, 4, 4) sts at beg of next 3 RS rows, then 4 (2, 3, 4, 5) sts at beg of following RS row.

RIGHT FRONT

With A, cast on 37 (45, 45, 53, 53) sts.

Work even in Mosaic pat for 3 inches, ending with a WS row.

SHAPE WAIST

Dec 1 st at end of next row, and then [every 16 rows] twice. (34, 42, 42, 50, 50 sts)

Work even until piece measures approx 9½ (9¾, 9¾, 9¾, 9¾) inches from beg, ending with a WS row.

Inc 1 st at end of next row and then [every 12 rows] twice. (37, 45, 45, 53, 53 sts)

At the same time, when piece measures approx 11 (11½, 12, 12½, 12½) inches, ending with a WS row, shape neck as follows:

SHAPE NECK & ARMHOLE

Dec 1 st at beg of next row, then dec 1 st at neck edge [every 6 rows] 3 times, [every 8 rows] 9 times, and *at the same time*, when piece measures approx 15 inches from beg, bind off 4 (6, 8, 8, 10) sts at armhole edge once, then bind off 2 (2, 2, 3, 3) sts at armhole edge once, then dec 1 st at armhole edge [every row] 1 (3, 4, 6, 8) times, then [every other row] 4 (3, 3, 3, 2) times. (13, 14, 15, 16, 17 sts rem)

Work even in pat as established until piece measures same as back to shoulder, ending with a RS row.

SHAPE SHOULDER

Bind off 3 (4, 4, 4, 4) sts at beg of next 3 WS rows, then 4 (2, 3, 4, 5) sts at beg of following WS row.

SLEEVES

With A, cast on 45 sts.

Beg Mosaic pat, and inc 1 st each side on next row, then [every 12 rows] 0 (0, 3, 10, 10) times, [every 14 rows] 0 (0, 6, 0, 0) times, [every 18 rows] 0 (3, 0, 0, 0) times, [every 20 rows] 0 (3, 0, 0, 0) times, [every 26 rows] 3 (0, 0, 0, 0) times, then [every 28 rows] 1 (0, 0, 0, 0) times. (55, 59, 65, 67, 67 sts)

Work even until piece measures approx 18½ inches from beg.

SHAPE CAP

Bind off 4 (6, 8, 8, 10) sts at beg of next 2 rows, then dec 1 st each side [every 4 rows] 7 (9, 10, 11, 12) times, then [every other row] 6 (4, 4, 4, 2) times. (21 sts)

Bind off 2 sts at beg of next 4 rows.

Bind off 13 sts.

FINISHING

Block all pieces to finished measurements.

Sew shoulder seams.

FRONT EDGING

With RS facing and A, beg at lower left-front edge, pick up and knit 107 sts along left-front edge, 43 sts along back neck, and 107 sts down right-front edge. (257 sts)

Next row (WS): Knit.
Next row: Purl.

Bind off knitwise on WS.

Set in sleeves. Sew sleeve and side seams.

Weave in all ends. ∎

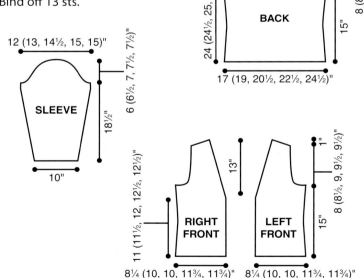

Cabled Wishes Pullover

Knit this classic pullover from the top down. It's completely seamless and easy to try on as you knit. The baby-cable trim is a pretty bonus!

Design by Debbie O'Neill

SKILL LEVEL
■■■□ INTERMEDIATE

SIZES
Women's extra-small (small, medium, large, extra-large, 2X-large) Instructions are given for smallest size, with larger sizes in parentheses. When only 1 number is given, it applies to all sizes.

FINISHED MEASUREMENTS
Bust: 34 (37, 40, 43½, 47, 49½) inches
Length: 20½ (21¾, 22¾, 24, 25½, 26) inches

MATERIALS
- **Featured yarn:** South West Trading Co. Karaoke 50 percent Soy Silk/50 percent wool worsted weight yarn (109 yds/50g per ball): 8 (9, 11, 13, 14, 15) balls lavender rose #294
- **Option yarn:** Moda Dea Washable Wool 100 percent merino super-wash wool worsted weight yarn (166 yd/100g per ball): 6 (7, 8, 9, 10, 11) balls true red #4490
- Size 7 (4.5mm) double-pointed and circular knitting needles (16, 24 and 29 inches long) or size needed to obtain gauge
- Stitch markers, 1 in CC for beg of rnd
- Scrap yarn
- Tapestry needle

GAUGE
20 sts and 28 rows = 4 inches/10cm in St st
To save time, take time to check gauge.

SPECIAL ABBREVIATIONS
Pm: Place marker
M1L (Make 1 Left): Insert LH needle from front to back under the horizontal lp between the last st worked and next st on LH needle. With RH needle, knit into the back of this lp.
M1R (Make 1 Right): Insert LH needle from back to front under the horizontal lp between the last st worked and next st on left needle. With RH needle, knit into the front of this lp.

SPECIAL TECHNIQUE
Cable cast on: *Knit into gap between last 2 sts on LH, place new st onto LH needle by slipping it knitwise; rep from *.

PATTERN STITCHES
A. Baby Cable (knit flat)
(multiple of 4 sts)
Rows 1 and 3 (WS): *K1, p2, k1; rep from * across.
Row 2 (RS): *P1, k2, p1; rep from * across.
Row 4: *P1, knit the 2nd st on LH needle and leave on needle, then knit the first st on LH needle and sl both sts off tog, p1; rep from * across.
Rep Rows 1–4 for pat.

B. Baby Cable (knit in round)
(multiple of 4 sts)
Rnds 1, 2, and 3: *P1, k2, p1; rep from * around.

Option

Rnd 4: *P1, knit the 2nd st on LH needle and leave on needle, then knit the first st on LH needle and sl both sts off tog, p1; rep from * around.

Rep Rnds 1–4 for pat.

PATTERN NOTES

This sweater is worked in 1 piece from the top down.

Change to larger or smaller circular needles (or to double-pointed needles) when sts no longer fit comfortably on needle being used.

BODY

Using 24-inch circular needle, cast on 52 (56, 61, 65, 75, 79) sts.

Set-up row 1 (WS): P1 [front], pm, p2 [raglan seam], pm, p10 (11, 12, 14, 15) [sleeve], pm, p2 [raglan seam], pm, p26 (29, 31, 37, 39) [back], pm, p2 [raglan seam], pm, p10 (11, 12, 14, 15) [sleeve], pm, p2 [raglan seam], p1.

Next row: K1, sl marker, *knit in front and back of next 2 sts, sl marker, knit to marker, sl marker; rep from * to last st, k1. (60, 64, 69, 73, 83, 87 sts)

Next row: Slipping markers, *purl to marker, work Baby Cable over next 4 sts; rep from * to last 2 sts, p2.

Raglan Inc row (RS): *Knit to marker, M1L, sl marker, work Baby Cable pat over next 4 sts, sl marker, M1R; rep from *, to last st, k1. (68, 72, 77, 81, 91, 95 sts)

Rep Raglan Inc row [every other row] once more, ending with a WS row. (76, 80, 85, 89, 99, 103 sts)

Neck Inc row (RS): K1, knit into st 2 rows below st on RH needle, continue working Raglan incs as before working to last st, knit 1 in row below the next st, k1. (86, 90, 95, 99, 109, 113 sts)

Rep Neck Inc row [every other row] 6 times, ending with a WS row. (146, 150, 155, 159, 169, 173 sts)

JOIN FRONT NECK

Next row (RS): Slipping markers, *knit to marker, M1L, work Baby Cable, M1R; rep from *, knit to end, then using cable cast-on method, cast on 8 (10, 13, 15, 21, 23) sts, pm for beg of rnd and join. (162, 168, 176, 182, 198, 204 sts)

Continue in pat at established, working inc before and after raglan markers [every other rnd] 15 (17, 19, 22, 24, 25) times. (282, 304, 328, 358, 390, 404 sts)

DIVIDE WORK

Dividing 4-st raglan seams between adjacent sections, sl 78

(84, 91, 99, 109, 113) front and back sts, and 63 (68, 73, 80, 86, 89) right sleeve sts to scrap yarn for holders.

SLEEVES

Transfer the rem 63 (68, 73, 80, 86, 89) left sleeve sts to 16-inch circular needle.

Starting at front edge of sleeve, cast on 4 (4, 4, 5, 4, 5) sts, then knit cast-on sts and sleeve sts; cast on 4 (4, 5, 5, 4, 6) sts, pm for center underarm and beg of rnd, and join. (70, 76, 82, 90, 94, 100 sts)

Work even in St st for 1 (1, 1, 1, 1½, 1½) inches.

Dec rnd: K1, ssk, knit to last 3 sts, k2tog, k1. (68, 74, 80, 88, 92, 98 sts)

Rep Dec rnd every 4 rnds 12 (15, 16, 20, 20, 23) times. (44, 44, 48, 48, 52, 52 sts)

Work even until sleeve measures 13½ (14, 15, 16, 16¾, 17½) inches from underarm, or 3 inches short of desired length.

Work Baby Cable pat for 3 inches.

Bind off loosely in pat.

Rep for right sleeve.

BODY

Place front and back sections sts on the longest circular needle. Join yarn and knit front sts, pick up and knit 7 (8, 9, 10, 8, 11) underarm sts from right sleeve, knit back sts, pick up and knit 7 (8, 9, 10, 8, 11) underarm sts from left sleeve; pm for beg of rnd and join. (170, 184, 200, 218, 234, 248 sts)

Work even in St st for 10 (10½, 11, 11½, 12, 12½) inches or 3 inches short of desired length, and on last rnd, dec 2 (0, 0, 2, 2, 0) sts evenly around. (168, 184, 200, 216, 232, 248 sts)

Work Baby Cable pat for 3 inches, ending with Rnd 1.

Bind off very loosely in pat.

FINISHING
NECK

Using 16-inch circular needle, pick up and knit 80 (84, 92, 100, 112, 120) sts around neck. Work in Baby Cable pat for approx 1 inch, ending with Rnd 1.

Bind off very loosely in pat.

Weave in all ends.

Block to finished measurements. ∎

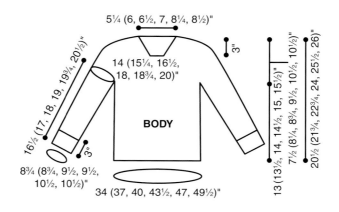

5¼ (6, 6½, 7, 8¼, 8½)"

14 (15¼, 16½, 18, 18¾, 20)"

3"

16½ (17, 18, 19, 19¾, 20½)"

BODY

8¾ (8¾, 9½, 9½, 10½, 10½)"

3"

34 (37, 40, 43½, 47, 49½)"

13 (13½, 14, 14½, 15, 15½)"

7½ (8¼, 8¾, 9½, 10½, 10½)"

20½ (21¾, 22¾, 24, 25½, 26)"

Dynamic Vest

Knit a stylish vest in colors that add life to your wardrobe. Choose an interesting yarn, and it does the color work for you.

Design by E. J. Slayton

SKILL LEVEL
■■■□ INTERMEDIATE

SIZES
Woman's small (medium, large, extra-large, 2X-large) Instructions are given for smallest size, with larger sizes in parentheses. When only 1 number is given, it applies to all sizes.

FINISHED MEASUREMENTS
Chest: 38 (42, 46, 50, 54) inches
Length: Approx 31 inches

Option

MATERIALS
- **Featured yarn:** South West Trading Co. Karaoke 50 percent Soy Silk/50 percent wool worsted weight yarn (109 yds/50g per ball): 8 (8, 9, 10, 11) balls wild cherry #280
- **Option yarn:** Moda Dea Cartwheel 100 percent wool worsted weight yarn (77 yds/50g per ball): 11 (12, 13, 14, 15) balls bronzeberry #9605
- Size 6 (4mm) needles or size needed to obtain gauge
- Stitch markers
- Stitch holders
- Tapestry needle

GAUGE
17 sts and 26 rows = 4 inches/10cm in pat with larger needles
  To save time, take time to check gauge.

SPECIAL ABBREVIATIONS
CDD (Central Double Decrease): Sl next 2 sts as if to k2tog, k1, p2sso.
K1B: K1 in row below next st on RH needle.
W/T (Wrap/Turn): Bring yarn to front, sl next st, take yarn to back, return sl st to LH needle, turn.

SPECIAL TECHNIQUES
Hiding short-row wraps: On RS, knit to st just before wrapped st, insert the needle under wrap and knitwise into st and knit st and wrap tog; on WS, purl to st just before wrapped st, insert the right needle from behind into back lp of wrap and place it on left needle then purl wrap and st tog.
3-Needle Bind Off: With RS tog and needles parallel, using a 3rd needle, knit tog a st from the front needle with 1 from the back. *Knit tog a st from the front and back needles, and sl the first st over the 2nd to bind off. Rep from * across, then fasten off last st.

PATTERN STITCH
Broken Rib (multiple of 4 sts + 2)
Row 1 (RS): Knit across.
Row 2: Purl across.
Row 3: K2, *p2, k2; rep from * across.
Row 4: P2, *k2, p2; rep from * across.
  Rep Rows 1–4 for pat.

PATTERN NOTES
Sl edge st purlwise wyif, take yarn to back between tips of needles.

When working shaping, keep 2 sts at each edge in St st, inc and dec 1 st in from edge

Shawl collar is shaped using short rows. When working past wrapped st in garter st, do not "hide wrap."

Read instructions carefully before starting; several areas of shaping are worked *at the same time.*

BACK
Cast on 84 (92, 100, 108, 116) sts.

BORDER
Row 1 (WS): Sl 1 k2, *p2, k2; rep from * to last 5 sts, p2, k3.
Row 2: Sl 1, k4, *p2, k2; rep from * to last 3 sts, k3.
Rows 3–7: Rep Rows 1 and 2, ending with Row 1.

BEG PAT
Row 1 (RS): Sl 1, knit across.
Row 2: Sl 1, k2, purl to last 3 sts, end k3.
Row 3: Sl 1, k4, *p2, k2; rep from * to last 3 sts, k3.
Row 4: Sl 1, *k2, p2; rep from * to last 3 sts, k3.

Rep Rows 1–4 until back measures approx 6 inches from beg, ending with Row 4. Cast on 1 st at each edge on last row; mark each end of row. (86, 94, 102, 110, 118 sts)

Beg with Row 1, work in Broken Rib for approx 1 inch, then dec 1 st at each edge [every 8 rows] 5 (4, 4, 4, 4) times. (76, 86, 94, 102, 110 sts)

Work even until back measures 15½ (15, 14½, 14½, 14) inches from beg, then inc 1 st at each edge [every 12th rows] twice. (80, 90, 98, 106, 114 sts)

Work even until back measures 20½ (20, 19½, 19½, 19) inches from beg, ending with a WS row.

SHAPE ARMHOLES
Maintaining pat, bind off 5 (6, 7, 11, 14) sts at beg of next 2 rows, then dec 1 st at each side [every other row] 5 (5, 6, 6, 6) times. (60, 68, 72, 72, 74 sts)

Work even in pat until armhole measures 9½ (10, 10½, 10½, 11) inches, ending with a WS row.

SHAPE SHOULDERS

Rows 1 and 2: Work to 5 (6, 7, 7, 7) sts from end, W/T.

Rows 3–6: Work to 5 (6, 6, 6, 6) sts from end, W/T. Place marker on each side of rem 30, 32, 34, 34, 36 neck sts.

Rows 7 and 8: Work to end of row, hiding all wraps. Leave all sts on holder.

LEFT FRONT

Cast on 41 (45, 49, 53, 57) sts.

BORDER

Row 1 (WS): *P2, k2; rep from * to last 5 sts, end p2, k3.

Row 2: Sl 1, k4, *p2, k2; rep from * across.

Rows 3–7: Rep Rows 1 and 2, ending with Row 1.

BEG PAT

Row 1 (RS): Sl 1, knit across.

Row 2: Purl to last 3 sts, end k3.

Row 3: Sl 1, k4, *p2, k2; rep from * across.

Row 4: P2, k2; rep from * to last 5 sts, end p2, k3.

Rep Rows 1–4 until front measures approx 6 inches from beg, ending with Row 4. Cast on 1 st at end of last row; mark end of row. (42, 46, 50, 54, 58 sts)

Beg with Row 1, work in Broken Rib for approx 1 inch, then dec 1 st at armhole edge (beg of RS row) [every 8th row] 5 (4, 4, 4, 4) times. (37, 42, 46, 50, 54 sts)

Work even until front measures 15½ (15, 14½, 14½, 14) inches from beg, then inc 1 st at armhole edge [every 12th row] twice. (39, 44, 48, 52, 56 sts)

At the same time, when front measures 19 inches, beg with

a RS row, place a marker in this row and beg neck shaping by dec 1 st at neck edge (end of RS row) [every other row] 2 (3, 4, 4, 4) times, then [every 4th row] 12 times.

Work until front measures 20½ (20, 19½, 19½, 19) inches from beg, ending with a WS row.

SHAPE ARMHOLE

At beg of row, bind off 5 (6, 7, 11, 14) sts, then dec 1 st at armhole edge [every other row] 5 (5, 6, 6, 6) times.

Maintaining established pat, continue neck shaping until 15 (18, 19, 19, 19) shoulder sts rem, then work even until front measures same as back to shoulder, ending with a RS row.

SHAPE SHOULDER

Row 1 (WS): Work in pat to 5 (6, 7, 7, 7) sts from armhole edge, W/T.

Rows 2 and 4: Work across in pat.

Row 3: Work in pat to 5 (6, 6, 6, 6) sts from previous turn, W/T.

Row 5: Work across all sts in pat, hiding wraps.

Place rem sts on holder.

RIGHT FRONT

Cast on 41 (45, 49, 53, 57) sts.

BORDER

Row 1 (WS): Sl 1, *k2, p2; rep from * across.

Row 2: *K2, p2; rep from * to last 5 sts, k5.

Rows 3–7: Rep Rows 1 and 2, ending with Row 1.

BEG PAT

Row 1 (RS): Knit across.

Row 2: Sl 1, k2, purl across.

Row 3: *K2, p2; rep from * to last 5 sts, p2, k3.

Row 4: Sl 1, *k2, p2; rep from * across.

Rep Rows 1–4 until front measures approx 6 inches from beg, ending with Row 4. Cast on 1 st at beg of last row; mark beg of row. (42, 46, 50, 54, 58 sts)

Beg with Row 1, discontinue garter-st edge and work in pat for approx 1 inch, then dec 1 st at armhole edge (end of RS row) [every 8th row] 5 (4, 4, 4, 4) times. (37, 42, 46, 50, 54 sts)

Work even in pat until front measures 15½ (15, 14½, 14½, 14) inches from beg, then inc 1 st at armhole edge [every 12th row] twice. (39, 44, 48, 52, 56 sts)

At the same time, when front measures 19 inches, beg with a RS row, place a marker in this row and shape neck by dec 1 st at neck edge (beg of RS row) [every other row] 2 (3, 4, 4, 4) times, then [every 4th row] 12 times.

Work even until front measures 20½ (20, 19½, 19½, 19) inches from beg, ending with a RS row.

SHAPE ARMHOLE

At beg of row, bind off 5 (6, 7, 11, 14) sts, then dec 1 st at armhole edge [every other row] 5 (5, 6, 6, 6) times.

Maintaining established pat, continue neck shaping until 15 (18, 19, 19, 19) shoulder sts rem, then work even until front measures same as back to shoulder, ending with a WS row.

SHAPE SHOULDER

Row 1 (RS): Work in pat to 5 (6, 7, 7, 7) sts from armhole edge, W/T.

Rows 2 and 4: Work across in pat.

Row 3: Work in pat to 5 (6, 6, 6, 6) sts from previous turn, W/T.

Row 5: Work across all sts in pat, hiding wraps.

Place rem sts on holder.

FINISHING

Block all pieces to finished measurements.

Bind off front and back shoulders, using 3-needle bind off.

FRONT BANDS & COLLAR

With RS facing, beg at bottom of right front, working at a rate of approx 3 sts for every 5 rows, pick up and knit 78 sts to beg of neck shaping, place marker; K1B, pick up and knit 40 sts along neck edge to shoulder, place marker; knit 30, 32, 34, 34, 36 neck sts, dec 3 sts evenly across (27, 29, 31, 31, 33 sts rem), place marker; pick up and knit 40 sts to beg of neck shaping, K1B, place marker; pick up and knit 78 sts to bottom of left front. (265, 267, 269, 269, 271 sts)

Row 1 (WS): Sl 1, knit across.

Row 2: Sl 1, knit to 1 st past 3rd marker (left shoulder), W/T.

Row 3: Sl 1, knit to 1 st past 2nd marker (right shoulder), W/T.

Row 4: Knit to 3 sts past previous turn (without hiding wrap when you pass it), W/T.

Row 5: Rep Row 4.

Row 6: Rep Row 4, inc 9 sts evenly across back neck. (36,

38, 40, 40, 42 sts between back neck markers)

Rows 7–19: Rep Row 4. (8 sts rem on each side before front neck markers)

Rows 20–27: Knit to 1 st past previous turn, W/T.

Row 28: Knit to end.

Rows 29, 30 and 32: Sl 1, knit across.

Rows 31 and 33: Sl 1, k1, k2tog, knit to last 4 sts, end ssk, k2.

Sl first st, removing markers as you work, bind off purlwise to 1 st before first marker, bind off knitwise across collar to 1 st past 4th marker, bind off purlwise to end.

ARMBANDS

With RS facing, beg at center underarm, pick up and knit 1 st in each bound-off underarm st, marking last underarm, then pick up and knit 3 sts for every 5 rows to shoulder, pick up and knit same number of sts to other underarm, pick up and knit 1 st in each bound-off underarm st, marking first underarm st picked up.

Rows 1 and 3: Sl 1, knit across.

Row 2: Sl 1, [knit to 1 st before marked st, CDD] twice, knit to end.

Bind off all sts purlwise, dec 1 st at each marker.

Beg at side markers, sew side seams. Block lightly. ∎

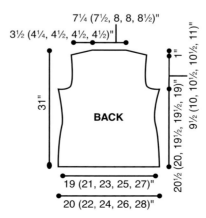

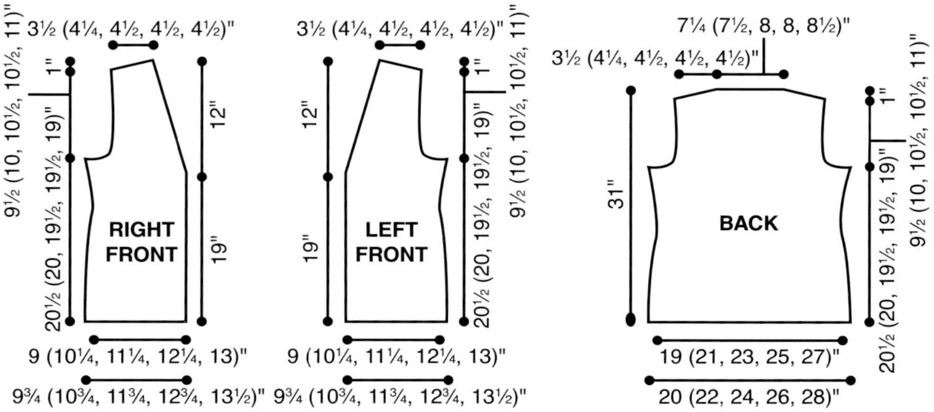

RIGHT FRONT

3½ (4¼, 4½, 4½, 4½)"

9½ (10, 10½, 10½, 11)"

1"

12"

19"

20½ (20, 19½, 19½, 19)"

9 (10¼, 11¼, 12¼, 13)"

9¾ (10¾, 11¾, 12¾, 13½)"

LEFT FRONT

3½ (4¼, 4½, 4½, 4½)"

12"

1"

9½ (10, 10½, 10½, 11)"

19"

20½ (20, 19½, 19½, 19)"

9 (10¼, 11¼, 12¼, 13)"

9¾ (10¾, 11¾, 12¾, 13½)"

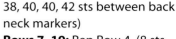

BACK

7¼ (7½, 8, 8, 8½)"

3½ (4¼, 4½, 4½, 4½)"

1"

9½ (10, 10½, 10½, 11)"

31"

20½ (20, 19½, 19½, 19)"

19 (21, 23, 25, 27)"

20 (22, 24, 26, 28)"

Classic Cables Vest

Make it light and bright for summer, or lush and tweedy for cooler weather. The choice is yours!

Design by Gayle Bunn

SKILL LEVEL

■■■□ INTERMEDIATE

SIZES

Woman's small (medium, large, extra-large, 2X-large) Instructions are given for smallest size, with larger sizes in parentheses. When only 1 number is given, it applies to all sizes.

FINISHED MEASUREMENTS

Chest: 37½ (40, 43½, 46, 48½) inches
Length: 21 (21½, 22, 22½, 23) inches

MATERIALS

- **Featured yarn:** Louet MerLin 70 percent merino/30 percent linen worsted weight yarn (156 yds/100g per skein): 4 (4, 5, 6, 6) skeins Goldilocks #05
- **Option yarn:** Red Heart McIntosh 70 percent acrylic/30 percent wool worsted weight yarn (122 yds/50g per ball): 6 (6, 7, 8, 8) balls merlot #1358
- Size 7 (4.5mm) knitting needles
- Size 8 (5mm) knitting needles or size needed to obtain gauge
- Cable needle
- Stitch holder
- Stitch markers

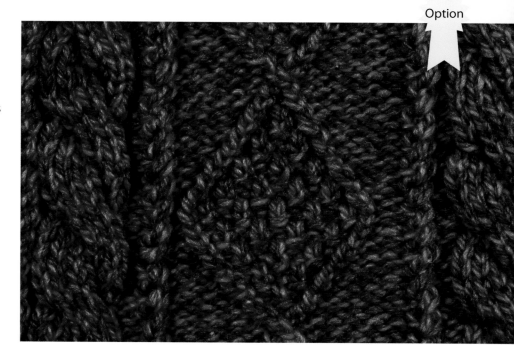

Option

- Safety pin
- Tapestry needle

GAUGE

19 sts and 25 rows = 4 inches/10cm in Irish Moss st with larger needles
To save time, take time to check gauge.

SPECIAL ABBREVIATIONS

T2R (Twist 2 Right): Knit into front of 2nd st on left-hand needle but do not drop st off needle, then knit into first st and sl both sts off needle.

C8F (Cable 8 Front): Sl 4 sts to cn and hold in front, k4, then k4 from cn.

Cr2F (Cross 2 Front): Sl next st to cn and hold in front, p1, then k1-tbl from cn.

Cr2B (Cross 2 Back): Sl next st to cn and hold in back, k1-tbl, the p1 from cn.

Cr3F (Cross 3 Front): Sl next st to cn and hold in front, k1-tbl into 2nd st on LH needle but do not drop st off needle, then purl into first st and sl both sts off needle, k1-tbl from cn.

PATTERN STITCHES

A. Irish Moss (multiple of 2 sts +1)
Row 1 (RS): *K1, p1; rep from * to last st, k1.
Row 2: *P1, k1; rep from * to last st, p1.
Row 3: *P1, k1; rep from * to last st, p1.
Row 4: *K1, p1; rep from * to last st, k1.
Rep Rows 1–4 for pat.

B. Cable Panel A (12-st panel)
Row 1 (RS): P2, k8, p2.
Row 2 and all WS rows: K2, p8, k2.
Row 3: P2, C8F, p2.
Rows 5 and 7: Rep Row 1.
Row 8: Rep Row 2.
Rep Rows 1–8 for Cable Panel A.

C. Cable Panel B (15-st panel)
Row 1 (RS): P6, Cr3F, p6.
Row 2: K6, p1-tbl, k1, p1-tbl, k6.
Row 3: P5, Cr2B, k1, Cr2F, p5.
Row 4: K5, p1-tbl, k1, p1, k1, p1-tbl, k5.
Row 5: P4, Cr2B, k1, p1, k1, Cr2F, p4.
Row 6: K4, p1-tbl, [k1, p1] twice, k1, p1-tbl, k4.
Row 7: P3, Cr2B, [k1, p1] twice, k1, Cr2F, p3.
Row 8: K3, p1-tbl, [k1, p1] 3 times, k1, p1-tbl, k3.
Row 9: P2, Cr2B, [k1, p1] 3 times, k1, Cr2F, p2.
Row 10: K2, p1-tbl, [k1, p1] 4 times, k1, p1-tbl, k2.
Row 11: P1, Cr2B, [k1, p1] 4 times, k1, Cr2F, p1.
Row 12: K1, p1-tbl, [k1, p1] 5 times, k1, p1-tbl, k1.
Row 13: P1, Cr2F, [p1, k1] 4 times, p1, Cr2B, p1.
Row 14: Rep Row 10.
Row 15: P2, Cr2F, [p1, k1] 3 times, p1, Cr2B, p2.
Row 16: Rep Row 8.
Row 17: P3, Cr2F, [p1, k1] twice, p1, Cr2B, p3.
Row 18: Rep Row 6.
Row 19: P4, Cr2F, p1, k1, p1, Cr2B, p4.
Row 20: Rep Row 4.
Row 21: P5, Cr2F, p1, Cr2B, p5.
Row 22: Rep Row 2.
Rep Rows 1–22 for Cable Panel B.

FRONT

With smaller needles, cast on 90 (98, 102, 106, 110) sts.
Row 1 (RS): K2, *p2, k2; rep from * to end.
Row 2: P2, *k2, p2; rep from * to end.
Work even in rib until piece measures 2¾ inches, ending with a WS row, and on last row, inc 9 (9, 13, 17, 21) sts evenly across. (99, 107, 115, 123, 131 sts)
Change to larger needles.
Row 1 (RS): [K1, p1] 5 (7, 9, 11, 13) times, p2, (T2R, work Row 1 of Cable Panel A) twice, T2R, work Row 1 of Cable Panel B, [T2R, work Row 1 of Cable Panel A] twice, T2R, p2, [p1, k1] 5 (7, 9, 11, 13) times.
Row 2: [P1, k1] 5 (7, 9, 11, 13) times, k2, [p2, work Cable Panel A] twice, p2, work Cable Panel B, [p2, work Cable Panel A] twice, p2, k2, [k1, p1] 5 (7, 9, 11, 13) times.
Row 3: [P1, k1] 5 (7, 9, 11, 13) times, p2, (T2R, work Cable Panel A] twice, T2R, work Cable Panel B, [T2R, work Cable Panel A] twice, T2R, p2, [k1, p1] 5 (7, 9, 11, 13) times.
Row 4: [K1, p1] 5 (7, 9, 11, 13) times, k2, [p2, work Cable Panel A) twice, p2, work Cable Panel B, [p2,

work Cable Panel A] twice, p2, k2, [p1, k1] 5 (7, 9, 11, 13) times.
Work even in pats as established with Irish Moss at sides until piece measures approx 12½ inches, ending with Row 22 of Cable Panel B.

SHAPE ARMHOLES & V-NECK
Bind off 5 (7, 8, 9, 10) sts at beg next 2 rows. (89, 93, 99, 105, 111 sts)
Next row (RS): K1, ssk, work 41 (43, 46, 49, 52) sts in pat as established, sl center st onto a safety pin, with 2nd ball of yarn, work in pat as established to last 3 sts, k2tog, k1.
Next row: Working both sides *at the same time* with separate balls of yarn, p2, work to last 2 sts, p2.
Next row: K1, ssk, work in pat to 2 sts before neck edge, k2tog; ssk, work to last 3 sts, k2tog, k1.
Rep last 2 rows 4 (5, 6, 7, 8) times more. (34, 34, 35, 36, 37 sts each side)
Keeping 2 sts at armhole edges in St st, continue to dec 1 st at each neck edge [every other row] 6 (4, 5, 6, 4) times, then [every 4 rows] 5 (6, 6, 5, 6) times. (23, 24, 24, 25, 27 sts)

Work even until armhole measures 8 (8½, 9, 9½, 10) inches, ending with a WS row.

SHAPE SHOULDER

Bind off 11 (12, 12, 12, 13) sts at beg of next 2 rows, then bind off rem 12 (12, 12, 13, 14) sts at beg of following 2 rows.

BACK

With smaller needles, cast on 90 (98, 102, 106, 110) sts.

Work K2, P2 Rib as for front until piece measures 2¾ inches, ending with a WS row, and on last row, dec 1 (dec 3, inc 1, inc 3, inc 5) sts evenly across. (89, 95, 103, 109, 115 sts)

Change to larger needles.

Work even in Irish Moss until piece measures same as front to armhole, ending with a WS row.

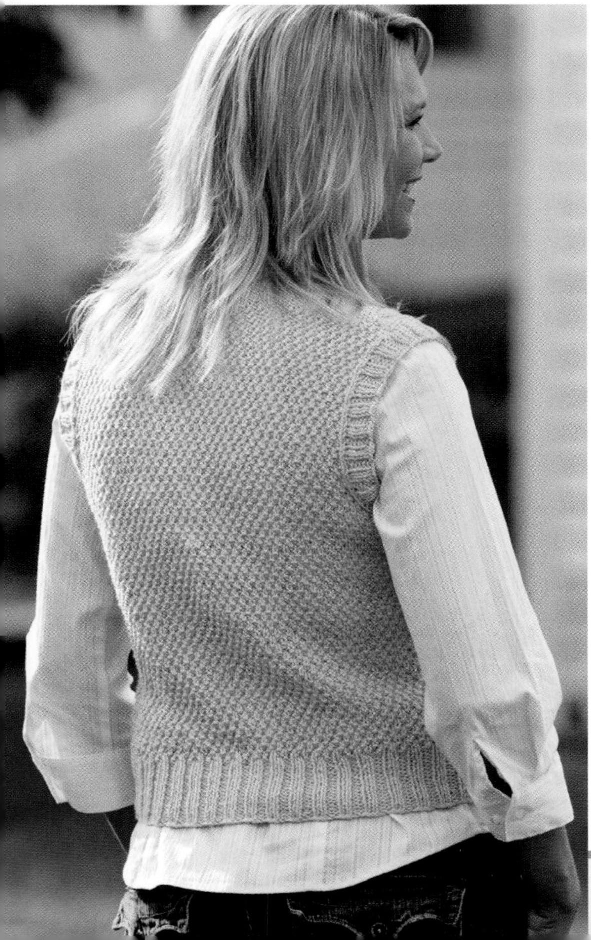

SHAPE ARMHOLES

Bind off 5 (7, 8, 9, 10) sts at beg of next 2 rows. (79, 81, 87, 91, 95 sts)

Next row (RS): K1, ssk, work pat as established to last 3 sts, k2tog, k1. (77, 79, 85, 89, 93 sts)

Next row: P2, work pat as established to last 2 sts, p2.

Rep last 2 rows 4 (5, 6, 7, 8) times more. (69, 69, 73, 75, 77 sts)

Maintaining first and last 2 sts in St st, work even in pat as established until armhole measures same as Front to beg of shoulder shaping, ending with a WS row.

SHAPE SHOULDERS

Bind off 10 (10, 11, 11, 11) sts at beg of next 2 rows, then bind off 11 (11, 11, 11, 12) sts at beg of following 2 rows.

Sl rem 27 (27, 29, 31, 31) sts to a holder for back neck.

FINISHING

Block all pieces to finished measurements.

Sew right shoulder seam.

NECKBAND

With RS facing and smaller needles, pick up and knit 54 (58, 58, 62, 66) sts down left-front neck edge, place marker, p1 from center st safety pin, place marker, pick up and knit 54 (58, 58, 62, 66) sts up right-front neck edge, knit across 27 (27, 29, 31, 31) sts from back st holder, dec 1 (1, 3, 1, 1) st(s) evenly across. (135, 143, 143, 155, 163 sts)

Row 1 (WS): *K2, p2; rep from * to marker, k1, *p2, k2; rep from * to last 2 sts, p2.

Row 2: Slipping markers, work in rib as established to 2 sts before marker, k2tog, p1, ssk, work in rib to end.

Row 3: Work in rib as established to 2 sts before marker, k2tog, k1, ssk, work in rib to end.

Rep last 2 rows twice more, then bind off in rib, dec in center as before.

Sew left shoulder and neckband seam.

ARMBANDS

With RS facing and smaller needles, pick up and knit 94 (102, 110, 118, 126) sts evenly along armhole edge.

Work 5 rows of K2, P2 Rib.

Bind off in ribbing.

Sew side seams.

Weave in all ends. ■

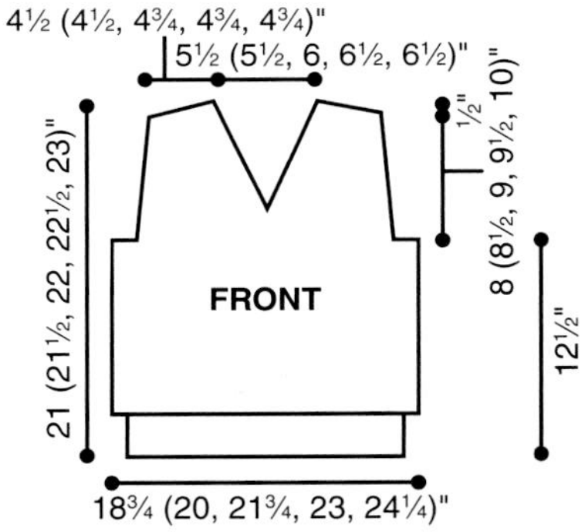
4½ (4½, 4¾, 4¾, 4¾)"
5½ (5½, 6, 6½, 6½)"
½"
8 (8½, 9, 9½, 10)"
12½"
21 (21½, 22, 22½, 23)"
FRONT
18¾ (20, 21¾, 23, 24¼)"

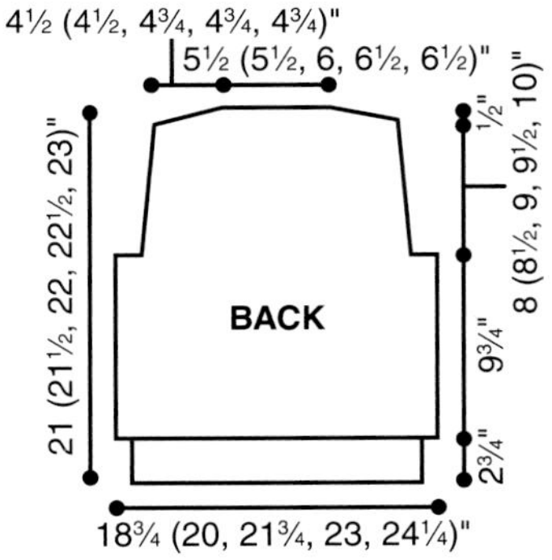
4½ (4½, 4¾, 4¾, 4¾)"
5½ (5½, 6, 6½, 6½)"
½"
8 (8½, 9, 9½, 10)"
9¾"
2¾"
21 (21½, 22, 22½, 23)"
BACK
18¾ (20, 21¾, 23, 24¼)"

Chain Reaction

Think comfort and easy-knitting in a timeless year-round shade of yarn like denim or rose. Wear it with a shirt when it's cool or without a shirt in summer.

Design by Shari Haux

SKILL LEVEL

 EASY

SIZES

Woman's small (medium, large, extra-large, 2X-large) Instructions are given for smallest size, with larger sizes in parentheses. When only 1 number is given, it applies to all sizes.

FINISHED MEASUREMENTS

Chest: Approx 36 (40, 44, 48, 52) inches
Length: 20½ (22¼, 24½, 25, 25) inches

MATERIALS

- **Featured yarn:**
  Plymouth Fantasy Naturale 100 percent cotton worsted weight yarn (140 yds/100g per skein): 7 (8, 8, 9, 10) skeins denim #9002
- **Option yarn:** N.Y. Yarns Olympic 70 percent acrylic/30 percent wool worsted weight yarn (130 yds/50g per ball): 8 (9, 9, 10, 11) balls rose #03
- Size 6 (4mm) circular needle

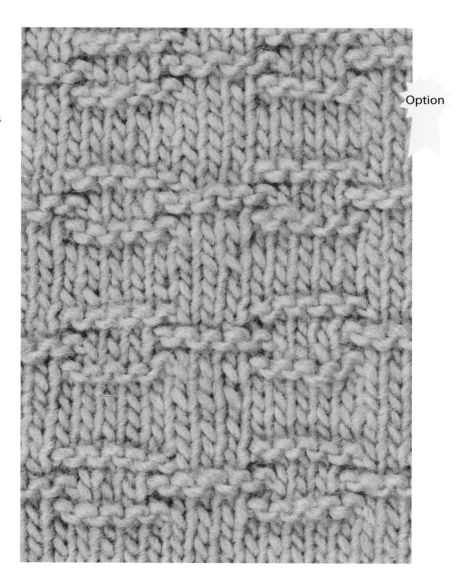

Option

- Size 8 (5mm) circular needle or size needed to obtain gauge
- Stitch markers
- Stitch holders
- Tapestry needle

GAUGE

16 sts and 26 rows = 4 inches/10cm in pat with larger needles

To save time, take time to check gauge.

SPECIAL TECHNIQUE

3-Needle Bind Off

With RS tog and needles parallel, using a 3rd needle, knit tog a st from the front needle with 1 from the back. *Knit tog a st from the front and back needles, and sl the first st over the 2nd to bind off. Rep from * across, then fasten off last st.

PATTERN STITCH

Chain Pat (multiple of 8 sts + 9)

Row 1 (RS): Knit.

Rows 2, 4, 6 and 8: Purl.

Row 3: Knit.

Row 5: K2, *p5, k3; rep from * to last 7 sts, p5, k2.

Row 7: P2, *p1, k3, p4; rep from * to last 7 sts, p1, k3, p1, p2.

Row 9: Rep Row 5.

Row 10: Purl.

Rep Rows 1–10 for pat.

BACK

With smaller needle, cast on 73 (81, 89, 97, 105) sts. Knit 13 (13, 13, 15, 15) rows (garter st), ending with a WS row.

Change to larger needle and [work pat Rows 1–10] 7 (8, 9, 9, 9) times ending with Row 10. Work 4 rows garter st.

Row 1 (RS): Knit across, place marker, cast on 8 sts.

Row 2: K7, p1, knit to end of row, place marker, cast on 8 sts. (89, 97, 105, 113, 121 sts)

Row 3: K7, sl 1, knit to marker, sl 1, k7.

Row 4: K7, p1, knit to marker, p1, k7.

Rep Rows 3 and 4 until yoke measures approx 8 (8½, 9, 9½, 9½) inches, ending with a RS row.

SHAPE NECK

K28 (32, 36, 39, 43), sl to holder; bind off center 33 (33, 33, 35, 35) sts; knit rem sts and sl to holder.

FRONT

Work as for back until yoke/sleeve area measures 3 (3, 3, 4, 4) inches less than back to shoulder.

SHAPE NECK

K39 (43, 47, 50, 54); attach 2nd ball of yarn, bind off center 11 (11, 11, 13, 13) sts, knit rem sts.

Continue to work both sides at once, binding off at each neck edge [2 sts] 3 times, then [1 st] 5 times. (28, 32, 36, 39, 43 sts rem)

Work even on rem sts until front yoke measures same as back.

FINISHING

Block both pieces to finished measurements.

Join front and back shoulders using 3-needle bind off.

NECKBAND

With RS facing and using smaller circular needle, beg at left shoulder seam, pick up and knit 54 (54, 54, 60, 60) sts evenly around neck edge to right shoulder, and 20 (20, 20, 24, 24) sts across back neck. Place marker and join to work in rnds. (74, 74, 74, 84, 84 sts)

Rnd 1: Knit.

Rnds 2 and 3: Purl.

Bind off all sts purlwise.

Sew side seams.

Weave in all ends. ■

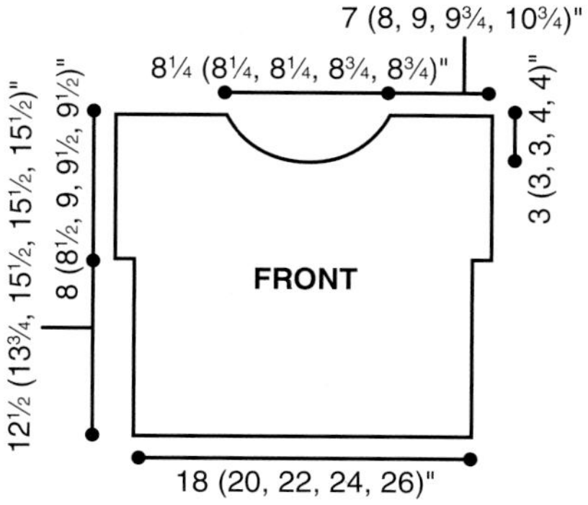
7 (8, 9, 9¾, 10¾)"
8¼ (8¼, 8¼, 8¾, 8¾)"
3 (3, 3, 4, 4)"
12½ (13¾, 15½, 15½, 15½)"
8 (8½, 9, 9½, 9½)"
FRONT
18 (20, 22, 24, 26)"

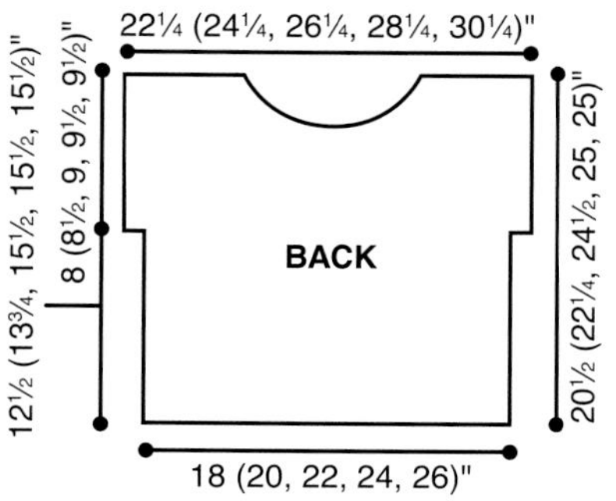
22¼ (24¼, 26¼, 28¼, 30¼)"
12½ (13¾, 15½, 15½, 15½)"
8 (8½, 9, 9½, 9½)"
20½ (22¼, 24½, 25, 25)"
BACK
18 (20, 22, 24, 26)"

Marvelous Afghans & Pillows

Of course you'll want to make afghans to warm up the corners of your family room and to have handy on your family's favorite reading and relaxing chairs. You'll also enjoy making quick pillows to update your surroundings.

Pleasure Colors

What's your pleasure? Whether you choose bright dynamic hues or soft soothing shades of green and brown, you'll enjoy relaxing as you knit this afghan.

Design by Kathy Wesley

SKILL LEVEL
■■□□ EASY

FINISHED SIZE
Approx 46 x 60 inches

MATERIALS
• **Featured yarn:** Lion Brand Yarn Lion Wool 100 percent wool worsted weight yarn (158 yds/85g per ball): 4 balls rose #140 (A); 2 balls each goldenrod #187 (B), purple #147 (C), lemongrass #132 (D) and pumpkin #133 (E)

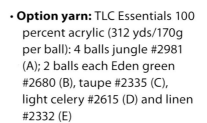

• **Option yarn:** TLC Essentials 100 percent acrylic (312 yds/170g per ball): 4 balls jungle #2981 (A); 2 balls each Eden green #2680 (B), taupe #2335 (C), light celery #2615 (D) and linen #2332 (E)
• Size 8 (5mm) 29-inch circular needle or size needed to obtain gauge
• Size G/6 (4mm) crochet hook
• Tapestry needle

GAUGE
15 sts and 30 rows = 4 inches/10cm in garter st

To save time, take time to check gauge.

PATTERN NOTES
Circular needle used to accommodate sts; do not join, work back and forth in rows.

Cut each yarn when you change colors; do not carry up sides.

AFGHAN
With A, cast on 176 sts.
Rows 1 (RS)–4: With A, knit.
Row 5: With B, knit.
Rows 6 and 7: P1, *yo, p2tog; rep from * to last st, p1.
Row 8: Purl.
Rows 9–12: Rep Rows 5–8.
Rows 13–16: Rep Rows 1–4.
Rows 17–24: With C, [rep Rows 5–8] twice.
Rows 25–28: Rep Rows 1–4.
Rows 29–36: With D, [rep Rows 5–8] twice.
Rows 37–40: Rep Rows 1–4.
Rows 41–48: With E, [rep Rows 5–8] twice.
Rep Rows 1–48 until piece measures approx 60 inches, ending with a rep of Rows 1–4.
Bind off knitwise.
Weave in all ends. ∎

Option

Dashing Hues

It certainly is dramatic how this afghan changes in feel by just changing the colors!

Design by Sandy Scoville

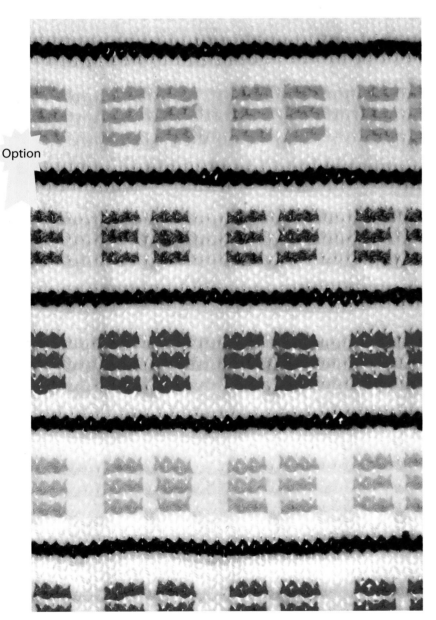

Option

SKILL LEVEL
◼◼◻◻ EASY

FINISHED SIZE
Approx 44 x 60 inches

MATERIALS
- **Featured yarn:** Moda Dea Fashionista 50 percent acrylic/50 percent Tencel/Lyocell) worsted weight yarn (183 yds/100g per ball): 7 balls black #6112 (MC), 3 balls ivory #6113 (A), 1 ball each olive #6122 (B) and boysenberry #6131 (C)
- **Option yarn:** Assorted worsted weight yarns (210 yds/90g per skein): 9 skeins off-white (MC), 2 skeins blue (A) and 1 skein each of 5 different colors*
- Size 8 (5mm) circular knitting needle or size needed to obtain gauge
- Tapestry needle

*Option afghan swatch was made with 1 yarn for main color, a 2nd color for the stripe and 5 assorted colors for dashes of color.

GAUGE
20 sts and 26 rows = 4 inches/ 10cm in St st (knit 1 row, purl 1 row)

To save time take time to check gauge.

PATTERN NOTES

Circular needle used to accommodate sts; do not join, work back and forth in rows.

Carry MC loosely along side edge when not in use.

Sl all sts purlwise with yarn held to WS. When working on WS, after slipping sts, it will be necessary to move yarn under needle to back of work to be in position to knit the following sts.

AFGHAN

With MC, cast on 185 sts.

BOTTOM BORDER

Rows 1 (RS)–10: Knit.

BODY

Rows 1 and 3 (RS): With MC, knit.

Rows 2 and 4: Purl.

Rows 5 and 6: With B, knit.

Rows 7–10: With MC, rep Rows 1–4.

Rows 11 and 12: With A, k1, sl 3, *k3, sl 1, k3, sl 3; rep from * to last st, k1.

Rows 13 and 14: With MC, rep Rows 1 and 2.

Rows 15 and 16: With A, rep Rows 11 and 12.

Rows 17 and 18: With MC, rep Rows 1 and 2.

Rows 19 and 20: With A, rep Rows 11 and 12.

Rows 21–24: With A, rep Rows 1–4.

Rows 25 and 26: With C, rep Rows 5 and 6.

Rows 27–40: Rep Rows 7–20.
  [Rep Rows 1–40] 8 times.
  Rep Rows 1–10.

TOP BORDER

Knit 9 rows.
  Bind off knitwise.

SIDE BORDER

With RS facing and using MC, pick up and knit 220 sts evenly spaced along 1 long edge.

Rows 1–9: Knit.
  Bind off knitwise.
  Rep on other long side.
  Weave in all ends. ■

Stadium Blanket

Knit with just one color for the background, then weave in contrasting yarns through the eyelets to make the plaid design. It's a great high school or college look!

Design by Diane Zangl

SKILL LEVEL

■■■□ INTERMEDIATE

FINISHED SIZE
Approx 44 x 44 inches
(excluding fringe)

MATERIALS
- **Featured yarn:** Caron Simply Soft 100 percent acrylic worsted weight yarn (330 yds/6 oz per skein): 4 skeins gray heather #9742 (MC), 1 skein each rubine red #9748 (B), off-white #9702 (C) and black #9727 (D)
- **Option yarn:** Plymouth Galway Worsted Colornep 93 percent wool/7 percent polyester worsted weight yarn (210 yds/100g per ball): 6 balls olive #527 (MC)
- Plymouth Galway Worsted 100 percent wool worsted weight yarn (210 yds/100g per ball): 1 ball each blue #164 (B), magenta #141 (C) and purple #132 (D)
- Size 6 (4mm) 29-inch circular needle or size needed to obtain gauge
- Long tapestry needle

Option

GAUGE

18 sts and 28 rows = 4 inches/10cm in pat st

To save time, take time to check gauge.

PATTERN NOTES

Circular needle used to accommodate sts; do not join; work back and forth in rows.

Do not tie fringe ends until all yarns have been woven through holes.

A chart is provided for the st pat.

BLANKET

With MC, cast on 204 sts.

Purl 1 row.

Row 1 (RS): Sl 1 knitwise wyib, then referring to chart, [work from A–C] 8 times, [work from A–B] once, end k1.

Row 2: Sl 1 purlwise wyif, [work from B–A] once, [work from C–A] 8 times, p1.

Working first and last sts as above, continue working pat from chart in this manner until Rows 1–36 have been repeated 8 times, then work [Rows 1–18] once.

Blanket should measure approx 45 inches.

Bind off all sts.

Block.

WOVEN DESIGN

Cut strands of yarn, each 65 inches long. You will need 88 each of B and C and 80 of D.

Weave 4 strands of yarn through all eyelet holes running vertically, working from left-to-right, in the following sequence: B, C, D.

Weave 4 strands of yarn through all eyelet holes running horizontally, working from bottom-to-top, in the same sequence.

Adjust trailing yarn ends evenly; to maintain elasticity of blanket, do not pull strands too tight. Tie 2 groups of adjacent strands in an overhand knot.

Trim fringe even.

Reblock. ■

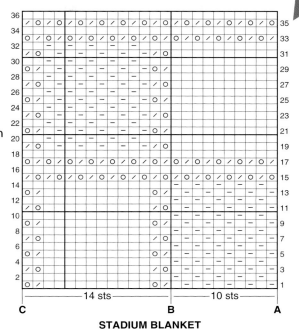

STITCH KEY
- ☐ K on RS, p on WS
- – P on RS, k on WS
- ⊙ Yo
- ╱ K2tog

STADIUM BLANKET

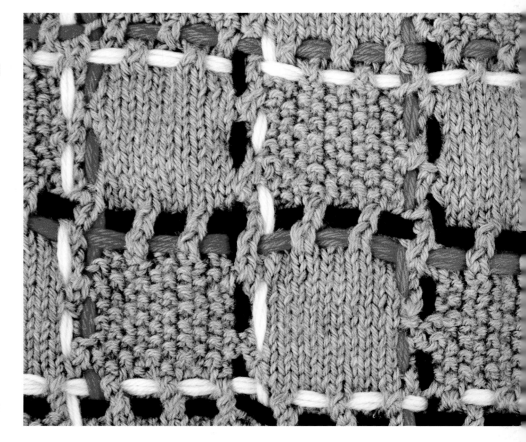

Woven Splendor

Use two coordinating shades of yarn for a designer-look afghan or use a dozen different colors on a neutral main color.

Design by Sandy Scoville

SKILL LEVEL
■■□□ EASY

FINISHED SIZE
Approx 40 x 52 inches

MATERIALS
- **Featured yarn:** Red Heart Plush 80 percent acrylic/20 percent nylon worsted weight yarn (278 yds/170g per skein): 3 skeins eggplant #9534 (MC) and 2 skeins light teal #9521 (CC)

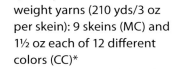

- **Option yarn:** Assorted worsted weight yarns (210 yds/3 oz per skein): 9 skeins (MC) and 1½ oz each of 12 different colors (CC)*
- Size 8 (5mm) 29-inch circular knitting needle
- Tapestry needle

*Option afghan swatch was made with 1 yarn for MC and 12 different colors for CC.

GAUGE
16 sts and 21 rows = 4 inches/10cm In St st

To save time, take time to check gauge.

PATTERN NOTES
Carry MC loosely along side edge when not in use.

Circular needle used to accommodate sts; do not join, work back and forth in rows.

Sl all sts purlwise with yarn held to WS. When working on WS, after slipping sts, it will be necessary to move yarn under needle to back of work to be in position to knit the following sts.

AFGHAN
With MC, cast on 184 sts.

BOTTOM BORDER
Rows 1 (RS)–4: Knit.

BODY
Row 1 (RS): With MC, knit.
Row 2: Purl.
Rows 3 and 4: With CC, k4; *sl 2, k4; rep from * across.
Row 5: With MC, knit.
Row 6: Purl.
Rows 7 and 8: With CC, k1, sl 2; *k4, sl 2; rep from * to last st, k1.

Rep Rows 1–8 until afghan measures approx 51 inches, ending with Row 2.

TOP BORDER
With MC, knit 5 rows.
Bind off.

SIDE BORDER
With RS facing and using MC, pick up and knit 220 sts evenly spaced along 1 long side.
Knit 4 rows.
Bind off.
Rep on other long side.
Weave in all ends. ■

Option

Diamond Twist Afghan

This classic afghan makes a room seem more inviting. The lacy pattern makes it interesting to knit and enjoy!

Design by Kathy Wesley

SKILL LEVEL

 INTERMEDIATE

Option

FINISHED SIZE

Approx 42 x 52 inches (excluding fringe)

MATERIALS

- **Featured yarn:**
  Plymouth Encore Worsted 75 percent acrylic/25 percent wool worsted weight yarn (200 yds/100g per ball): 8 balls teal green #9401
- **Option yarn:** Universal Yarn Deluxe Worsted Tweed 100 percent wool worsted weight yarn (220 yds/100g per skein): 8 skeins lemon grape #04
- Size 10 (6mm) circular needle or size needed to obtain gauge
- Medium-size crochet hook
- Tapestry needle

4 MEDIUM

GAUGE

16 sts and 20 rows = 4 inches/10cm in St st
To save time, take time to check gauge.

PATTERN NOTES

Circular needle used to accommodate sts; do not join, work back and forth in rows.

A chart is included for Rows 1–24 of the pat for the body of the afghan for those preferring to work pat from a chart.

STITCH KEY

☐ K on RS, p on WS
─ K on WS, p on RS
╱ K2tog
╲ Ssk
◉ Yo
⋀ Sk2p

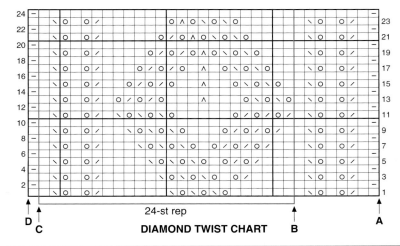

DIAMOND TWIST CHART

24-st rep

D C B A

AFGHAN
Cast on 153 sts.

LOWER BORDER
Row 1 (WS): K1, purl to last st, k1.
Row 2 (RS): K2, *k2tog, yo, k1, yo, ssk, k1; rep from * to last st, k1.
Rows 3–10: [Rep Rows 1 and 2] 4 times.
Row 11: Rep Row 1.

BODY
Row 1 (RS): K2, k2tog, yo, k1, yo, ssk, k1; *k6, [yo, ssk] 3 times, k6, k2tog, yo, k1, yo, ssk, k1; rep from * to last st, k1.
Row 2 and all WS rows: K1, purl to last st, k1.
Row 3: K2, k2tog, yo, k1, yo, ssk, k1; *k4, k2tog, yo, k1, [yo, ssk] 3 times, k5, k2tog, yo, k1, yo, ssk, k1; rep from * to last st, k1.
Row 5: K2, k2tog, yo, k1, yo, ssk, k1; *k3, [k2tog, yo] twice, k1, [yo, ssk] 3 times, k4, k2tog, yo, k1, yo, ssk, k1; rep from * to last st, k1.
Row 7: K2, k2tog, yo, k1, yo, ssk, k1; *k2, [k2tog, yo] 3 times, k1, [yo, ssk] 3 times, k3, k2tog, yo, k1, yo, ssk, k1; rep from * to last st, k1.
Row 9: K2, k2tog, yo, k1, yo, ssk, k1; *k1, [k2tog, yo] 3 times, k3, [yo, ssk] 3 times, k2, k2tog, yo, k1, yo, ssk, k1; rep from * to last st, k1.
Row 11: K2, k2tog, yo, k1, yo, ssk, k1; *[k2tog, yo] 3 times, k5, [yo, ssk] 3 times, k1, k2tog, yo, k1, yo, ssk, k1; rep from * to last st, k1.
Row 13: K2, k2tog, yo, k1, yo, ssk, k1; *[yo, ssk] twice, yo, k3, sk2p, k3, [yo, k2tog] twice, yo, k1, k2tog, yo, k1, yo, ssk, k1; rep from * to last st, k1.
Row 15: K2, k2tog, yo, k1, yo, ssk, k1; *k1, [yo, ssk] twice, yo, k2, sk2p, k2, [yo, k2tog] twice, yo, k2, k2tog, yo, k1, yo, ssk, k1; rep from * to last st, k1.
Row 17: K2, k2tog, yo, k1, yo, ssk, k1; *k2, [yo, ssk] twice, yo, k1, sk2p, k1, [yo, k2tog] twice, yo, k3, k2tog, yo, k1, yo, ssk, k1; rep from * to last st, k1.
Row 19: K2, k2tog, yo, k1, yo, ssk, k1; *k3, [yo, ssk] twice, yo, sk2p, [yo, k2tog] twice, yo, k4, k2tog, yo, k1, yo, ssk, k1; rep from * to last st, k1.
Row 21: K2, k2tog, yo, k1, yo, ssk, k1; *k4, [yo, ssk] twice, yo, sk2p, yo, k2tog, yo, k5, k2tog, yo, k1, yo, ssk, k1; rep from * to last st, k1.
Row 23: K2, k2tog, yo, k1, yo, ssk, k1; *k5, [yo, ssk] twice, yo, sk2p, yo, k6, k2tog, yo, k1, yo, ssk, k1; rep from * to last st, k1.
Row 24: K1, purl to last st, k1.

Rep Rows 1–24 until afghan measures approx 50 inches, ending with Row 24. Rep Rows 1 and 2.

UPPER BORDER
Row 1 (RS): K2, *k2tog, yo, k1, yo, ssk, k1; rep from * to last st, k1.
Row 2: K1, purl to last st, k1.
Rows 3–10: [Rep Rows 1 and 2] 4 times.
Bind off.

FRINGE
Cut 154 (25-inch) strands. *Fold 1 strand in half. With RS facing and beg at corner of 1 edge, use crochet hook to draw folded end from RS to WS. Pull loose ends through folded section. Draw knot up firmly.

Rep from *, placing 1 fringe in every other st along each short edge.

Trim even. ∎

Tranquil Pillow Trio

Nothing adds the feeling of comfort to a sofa or bed like some hand-knit pillows. Choose yarn to complement the color scheme and fit in with the season.

Design by Anita Closic

Option

SKILL LEVEL
 ■□□ EASY

FINISHED SIZE
Approx 16 x 16 inches

MATERIALS
• **Featured Yarn:**
Plymouth Fantasy Naturale 100 percent mercerized cotton worsted weight yarn (140 yds/100g per skein): 4 skeins each orange #7250 (A), aqua #8021 (B), and orange multi #9995 (C)

• **Option Yarn:** Plymouth Boku 95 percent wool/5 percent silk worsted weight yarn (99 yds/50g per ball): 5 balls each blue multi #7 (A), blue/magenta multi #12 (B) and olive/purple/orange multi #8 (C)

• Size 11 (8mm) needles or size needed to obtain gauge

• Size I/9 (5.5mm) crochet hook

• 16-inch square pillow form for each pillow

• 4 large buttons for Button Pillow

• Tapestry needle

GAUGE

8 sts and 14 rows = 4 inches/10cm in St st with 2 strands of yarn held tog

To save time, take time to check gauge.

PATTERN NOTES

Pillow is worked holding 2 strands of yarn tog throughout.

If working with option yarn, start both balls of yarn in same spot in color sequence to maintain striping effect; it is not critical if colors change at somewhat different spots on the different balls of yarn.

A. DIRECTIONAL STRIPE PILLOW

With 2 strands A held tog, cast on 32 sts.

*Rows 1–8: Work in St st (knit on RS, purl on WS).

Rows 10–18: Work in rev St st (purl on RS, knit on WS).

Rep Rows 1–18 twice more, then work Rows 1–8.

Bind off loosely, leaving last st on needle.*

Mark the RS of fabric.

Turn work, and with RS facing, pick up and knit 32 sts along side edge.

Rep from * to *, fastening off last st.

Weave in ends.

FINISHING

Center pillow form over knitted piece.

With RS facing and using mattress st, sew center back seam.

Work 1 row of sc along 2 open edges, pinching corners to create pleat for additional shaping.

B. BLOCKS PILLOW
FRONT

With 2 strands B held tog, cast on 34 sts.

Row 1 (RS): K17, p17.

Rep Row 1 for 8 inches.

Row 2: P17, k17.

Rep Row 2 for 8 inches.

Bind off loosely.

BACK

Work as for front.

FINISHING

Weave in ends.

With WS tog and using crochet hook, work 1 row sc to join 3 sides of squares.

Sl pillow form inside and finish row of sc to close 4th side, ch 1. Do not turn.

Next row: With RS still facing and working from left to right, sc around, join with sl st.

C. BUTTON PILLOW
FRONT & BACK

With 2 strands C held tog, cast on 32 sts.

Work in St st for 32 inches.

FLAP

Next row: Inc 1 st each end. (34 sts)

Work in rev St st for 5 inches.

Bind off loosely.

FINISHING

Weave in ends.

With RS facing and using mattress st, sew sides of pillow tog.

Insert pillow form.

Sew buttons to flap, then tack flap to front and sides of pillow. ∎

Magical Leaves

Combine a simple garter-lace stitch, a soft and colorful self-striping yarn and some knitted leaves. The result: a pleasing square throw to add color to any room.

Design by Christine L. Walter

SKILL LEVEL
■■■□ INTERMEDIATE

FINISHED SIZE
Approx 50 x 50 inches, excluding leaves

Option

MATERIALS
- **Featured yarn:** Patons SWS 70 percent wool/30 percent soy worsted weight yarn (110 yds/80g per ball): 16 balls natural geranium #70530 (MC) and 2 balls natural green #70605 (CC)
- **Option yarn:** Caron Simply Soft Shadows 100 percent acrylic worsted weight yarn (150 yds/3 oz per skein): 12 skeins opal twist #0008 (MC)
- **Option yarn:** Caron Simply Soft Heather 100 percent acrylic worsted weight yarn (250 yds/5 oz per skein): 1 skein woodland heather #9503 (CC)
- Size 9 (5.5mm) circular needle or size needed to obtain gauge
- Size 8 (5mm) knitting needles
- Tapestry needle

4 MEDIUM

GAUGE
14 sts and 28 rows = 4 inches/10cm in Garter Lace pat
   To save time, take time to check gauge.

PATTERN STITCH
Garter Lace (multiple of 2 sts)
Rows 1 (RS)–6: Knit.
Rows 7 and 9: *Yo, k2tog; rep from * to end.
Rows 8 and 10: *Yo, p2tog; rep from * to end.
Rep Rows 1–10 for pat.

PATTERN NOTES
This throw is made up of 4 smaller sections that are knit in a modular fashion; the edge of the final section is sewn to the first section's cast-on edge.

AFGHAN
FIRST SECTION
With larger needles and MC, cast on 86 sts.
Set-up row (RS): K2, work Row 1 of Garter Lace pat to last 2 sts, k2.
   Maintaining first and last 2 sts in Garter Lace pat, continue in pat for 176 rows, ending with Row 6 of pat.

With RS facing, bind off, leaving last st on needle; do not break yarn.

SECOND SECTION
Turn first section sideways.

With RS facing, pick up and knit 85 sts along left side of first section. (86 sts)

Beg with Row 2 of Garter Lace pat, work as for first section.

THIRD SECTION
Turn piece sideways.

With RS facing, pick up and knit 85 sts along left side of 2nd section. (86 sts)

Beg with Row 2 of Garter Lace pat, work as for first section.

LAST SECTION
Turn piece sideways.

With RS facing, pick up and knit 85 sts along left side of 3rd section. (86 sts)

Beg with Row 2 of Garter Lace pat, work as for first section, but bind off last st.

Cut yarn leaving a long tail for sewing.

With RS facing and using mattress st, sew side of last section to cast-on edge of first section to complete the square.

LEAF CLUSTERS
Note: *Use only the green and beige section of variegated yarn.*

LEAF BACK
Make 20
With smaller needles and CC, cast on 5 sts.

Row 1 (RS): K2, yo, k1, yo, k2. (7 sts)

Row 2 and all WS rows: Purl.

Row 3: K3, yo, k1, yo, k3. (9 sts)

Row 5: K4, yo, k1, yo, k4. (11 sts)

Row 7: Ssk, k7, k2tog. (9 sts)

Row 9: Ssk, k5, k2tog. (7 sts)

Row 11: Ssk, k3, k2tog. (5 sts)

Row 13: Ssk, k1, k2tog. (3 sts)

Row 15: Sk2p. (1 st)

Fasten off.

LEAF WITH STEM
Make 4
With smaller needles and CC, cast on 3 sts.

*K3, do not turn, sl sts back to LH needle; rep from * for I-cord stem until piece measures approx ¾ inch.

Inc 1 st each side, then turn and purl back. (5 sts)

Work Rows 1–15 of Leaf Back above.

With WS tog, sew 1 leaf back to each leaf with stem, then sew rem leaf backs to each other. You will have 4 leaves with stems and 8 leaves without stems.

Sew 1 plain leaf to each side of stem to form leaf clusters.

Sew 1 cluster to each corner of afghan.

FINISHING
Weave in ends. ■

Winning Waves

Ridges of texture and lace form lovely wavy stripes of color in this luxurious cotton afghan.

Design by Christine L. Walter

SKILL LEVEL

■■■□ INTERMEDIATE

FINISHED SIZE

Approx 40 x 48 inches

MATERIALS

- **Featured yarn:** S.R. Kertzer Super 10 Cotton 100 percent mercerized cotton worsted weight yarn (249 yds/125g per skein): 3 skeins butterscotch #3356 (MC), 2 skeins each champagne #3226 (CC1) and pear #3606 (CC2)
- **Option yarn:** Bernat Satin 100 percent acrylic worsted weight yarn (163 yds/100g per ball): 5 balls sultana #04307 (MC), 3 balls each star dust #04317 (CC1) and maitai #04732 (CC2)
- Size 9 (5.5mm) 40-inch circular needle or size needed to obtain gauge
- Size H/8 (5mm) crochet hook
- Tapestry needle

GAUGE

18 sts and 28 rows = 4 inches/10 cm in Wavy Lace

To save time, take time to check gauge.

SPECIAL ABBREVIATION

Kfb: Knit in front and back of st.

PATTERN STITCH

Wavy Lace (multiple of 11 sts + 1)

Row 1 (RS): K1, *k2tog, k2, kfb, k1, kfb, k2, k2tog-tbl; rep from * to end.

Rows 2, 4, and 6: Purl.

Rows 3 and 5: Rep Row 1.

Rows 7 and 8: Rep Row 2.

Row 10: P1, *yo, p2tog; rep from * to end.

Row 11: *K1-tbl, k1; rep from * to last st, k1.

Rows 12 and 13: Rep Row 2.

Option

Row 14: Purl.

Rep Rows 1-14 for pat using the color sequence given in pat instructions.

PATTERN NOTES

Wave Lace pat is worked between 3-st garter edges throughout.

Carry MC up side of piece; cut contrasting colors when each stripe is complete.

AFGHAN

With MC, cast on 183 sts.

Knit 2 rows.

Set-up row (RS): K3, work Row 1 of Wavy Lace pat, end k3.

Maintaining 3-st garter edges, continue working in pat following color sequence below:

With MC, work Rows 1–5.

With CC1, work Rows 6–13.

With MC, work Row 14.

With MC, work Rows 1–5.

With CC2, work Rows 6–13.

With MC, work Row 14.

Continue alternating contrast colors until 22 complete reps have been worked. (11 stripes in CC1 and 11 stripes in CC2)

Work Rows 1–5.

Knit 2 rows.

Bind off.

FINISHING

Weave in ends.

SIDE EDGES

Row 1 (RS): With MC and crochet hook, and beg at lower corner, work 158 sc evenly along long side, working sts between each garter ridge, ch 1, do not turn.

Row 2 (RS): Working from left to right, sc in each st to end, join with sl st. Rep on other side. ■

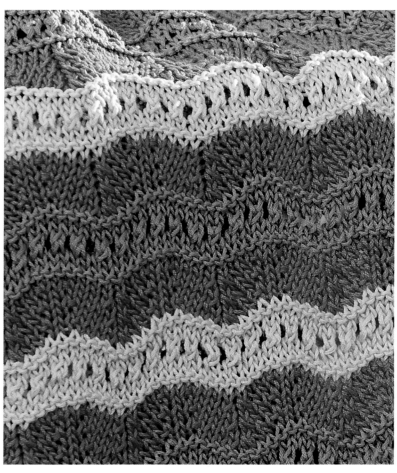

Vine Lace

This lacy beauty is knit in two pieces and then grafted together down the center. It would be stunning in most any color!

Design by Kennita Tully

SKILL LEVEL
■■■□ INTERMEDIATE

FINISHED SIZE
Approx 45 x 58 inches

MATERIALS
- **Featured yarn:**
  Plymouth Super Taj Majal 70 percent super fine merino/22 percent silk/8 percent cashmere worsted weight yarn (127 yds/50g per ball): 16 balls burnt orange #1436

- **Option yarn:** Plymouth Linen Isle 50 percent cotton/30 percent rayon/20 percent linen worsted weight yarn (86 yds/50g per ball): 24 balls aqua #8699
- Size 8 (5mm) 40-inch circular needle or size needed to obtain gauge
- Tapestry needle

GAUGE
19 sts and 23 rows = 4 inches/10cm in pat
  To save time, take time to check gauge.

PATTERN STITCH
Vine Lace (multiple of 9 sts + 4)

Rows 1 and 3 (WS): Purl.
Row 2 (RS): K3, *yo, k2, ssk, k2tog, k2, yo, k1; rep from * to last st, k1.
Row 4: K2, *yo, k2, ssk, k2tog, k2, yo, k1; rep from * to last 2 sts, k2.
  Rep Rows 1–4 for pat.

Option

PATTERN NOTES

Throw is made in 2 pieces and grafted down the middle.

Pat is worked back and forth; a circular needle is used to accommodate the large number of sts.

THROW

Make 2

Cast on 211 sts.

Work Vine Lace pat until piece measures approx 29 inches, ending with Row 3.

Sl all sts to a holder or another long circular needle to be grafted.

FINISHING

With RS facing, graft the 2 pieces tog using Kitchener st (see page 170).

Weave in all ends.

Block to finished measurements. ∎

Tempting Texture

If you'd like to give a gift afghan of heirloom quality, this is an outstanding choice. Choose a color to please the recipient or make it in a timeless neutral shade.

Design by Gayle Bunn

SKILL LEVEL
 EASY

FINISHED SIZE
Approx 43 x 55 inches

MATERIALS
- **Featured yarn:** Moda Dea Washable Wool 100 percent merino superwash wool worsted weight yarn (166 yd/100g per ball): 14 balls taupe #4435
- **Option yarn:** Patons Canadiana 100 percent acrylic worsted weight yarn (200 yd/100g per ball): 11 balls juniper #00052
- Size 8 (5mm) 36-inch circular needle or size needed to obtain gauge
- Cable needle
- Tapestry needle

GAUGE
24 sts and 25 rows = 4 inches in Trinity St
  To save time, take time to check gauge.

SPECIAL ABBREVIATIONS
C8B (Cable 8 Back): Sl next 4 sts to cn and hold in back, k4, k4 from cn.

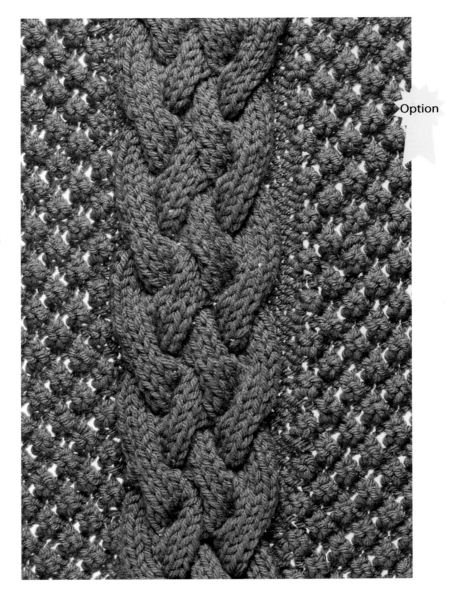

Option

C8F (Cable 8 Front): Sl next 4 sts to cn and hold in front, k4, k4 from cn.

PATTERN STITCHES

A. Trinity St (multiple of 4 sts + 2)
Row 1 (RS): Purl.
Row 2: K1, *(k1, p1, k1) all in next st, p3tog; rep from * to last st, k1.
Row 3: Purl.
Row 4: K1, *p3tog, *(k1, p1, k1) all in next st; rep from * to last st, k1.
    Rep Rows 1–4 for pat.

B. Cable Panel (24-st panel)
Row 1 (RS): P2, k20, p2.
Row 2 and all WS rows: K2, p20, k2.
Row 3: P2, k4, [C8F] twice, p2.
Rows 5 and 7: Rep Row 1.
Row 9: P2, [C8B] twice, k4, p2.
Row 11: Rep Row 1.
Row 12: Rep Row 2.
    Rep Rows 1–12 for pat.

PATTERN NOTE

Pat is worked back and forth; a circular needle is used to accommodate the large number of sts.

THROW

Cast on 198 sts.
    Starting with WS row, work 11 rows garter st (knit every row), and inc 68 sts evenly across last row. (266 sts)
Set-up row (RS): [Work 34 sts in Trinity St, work Cable Panel across next 24 sts] 4 times, work last 34 sts in Trinity St.
    Continue in pats as established until throw measures approx 53½ inches, ending with Row 12 of Cable Panel.
Next row (RS): Knit, dec 68 sts evenly across. (198 sts)

Work 10 rows garter st.
Bind off knitwise on WS.

FINISHING
SIDE EDGING

With RS facing, pick up and knit 246 sts evenly along side edge of throw.
    Work 10 rows garter st.
    Bind off knitwise on WS.
    Rep on opposite side edge.
    Weave in all ends. ■

Knitting Stitch Guide

A useful basic reference for you.

CAST ON

Leaving an end about an inch long for each stitch to be cast on, make a slip knot on the right needle.

Place the thumb and index finger of your left hand between the yarn ends with the long yarn end over your thumb and the strand from the skein over your index finger. Close your other fingers over the strands to hold them against your palm (Fig 1). Spread your thumb and index fingers apart and draw the yarn into a "V."

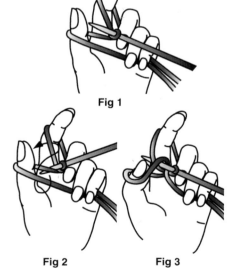

Fig 1

Fig 2   **Fig 3**

Place the needle in front of the strand around your thumb and bring it underneath this strand (Fig 2). Carry the needle over and under the strand on your index finger.

Draw through loop on thumb (Fig 3).

Drop the loop from your thumb and draw up the strand to form a stitch on the needle.

Repeat until you have cast on the number of stitches indicated in the pattern. Remember to count the beginning slip knot as a stitch.

CABLE CAST ON

This type of cast on is used when adding stitches in the middle or at the end of a row.

Make a slip knot on the left needle.

Knit a stitch in this knot and place it on the left needle.

Insert the right needle between the last two stitches on the left needle. Knit a stitch and place it on the left needle. Repeat for each stitch needed.

KNIT (K)

Insert tip of right needle from front to back stitch on left needle.

Bring yarn under and over the tip of the right needle.

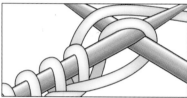

Pull yarn loop through the stitch with right needle point.

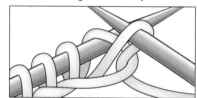

Slide the stitch off the left needle. The new stitch is on the right needle.

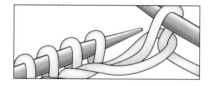

PURL (P)

With yarn in front, insert tip of right needle from back to front through next stitch on the left needle.

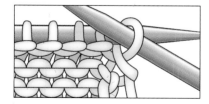

Bring yarn around the right needle counterclockwise.

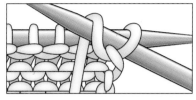

With right needle, draw yarn back through the stitch.

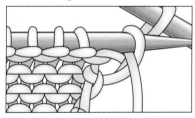

Slide the stitch off the left needle. The new stitch is on the right needle.

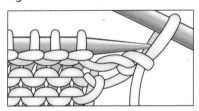

BIND OFF

Binding off (knit)

Knit first two stitches on left needle. Insert tip of left needle into first stitch worked on right needle and pull it over the second stitch and completely off the needle.

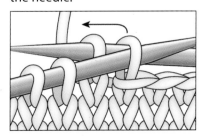

Knit the next stitch and repeat. When one stitch remains on right needle, cut yarn and draw tail through last stitch to fasten off.

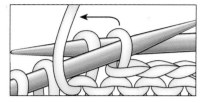

Binding off (purl)

Purl first two stitches on left needle. Insert tip of left needle into first stitch worked on right needle and pull it over the second stitch and completely off the needle.

Purl the next stitch and repeat. When one stitch remains on right needle, cut yarn and draw tail through last stitch to fasten off.

INCREASE (INC)

Two stitches in one stitch

Increase (knit)

Knit the next stitch in the usual manner, but don't remove the stitch from the left needle. Place right needle behind left needle and knit again into the back of the same stitch. Slip original stitch off left needle.

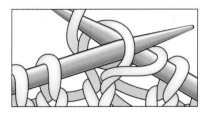

INCREASE (PURL)

Purl the next stitch in the usual manner, but don't remove the stitch from the left needle. Place right needle behind left needle

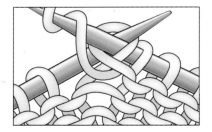

and purl again into the back of the same stitch. Slip original stitch off left needle.

INVISIBLE INCREASE (M1)

There are several ways to make or increase one stitch.

Make 1 with Left Twist (M1L)

Insert left needle from front to back under the horizontal loop between the last stitch worked and next stitch on left needle.

With right needle, knit into the back of this loop.

To make this increase on the purl side, insert left needle in same manner and purl into the back of the loop.

Make 1 with Right Twist (M1R)

Insert left needle from back to front under the horizontal loop between the last stitch worked and next stitch on left needle.

With right needle, knit into the front of this loop.

To make this increase on the purl side, insert left needle in same manner and purl into the front of the loop.

Make 1 with Backward Loop over the right needle
With your thumb, make a loop over the right needle.

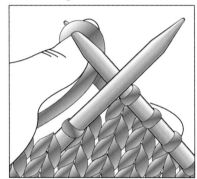

Slip the loop from your thumb onto the needle and pull to tighten.

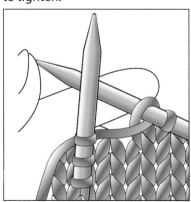

Make 1 in top of stitch below
Insert tip of right needle into the stitch on left needle one row below.

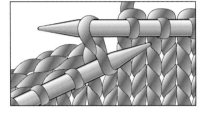

Knit this stitch, then knit the stitch on the left needle.

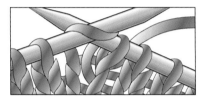

DECREASE (DEC)
Knit 2 together (k2tog)
Put tip of right needle through next two stitches on left needle as to knit. Knit these two stitches as one.

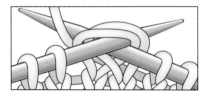

Purl 2 together (p2tog)
Put tip of right needle through next two stitches on left needle as to purl. Purl these two stitches as one.

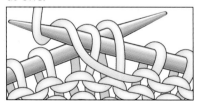

SLIP, SLIP, KNIT (SSK)
Slip next two stitches, one at a time, as to knit from left needle to right needle.

Insert left needle in front of both stitches and work off needle together.

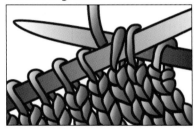

SLIP, SLIP, PURL (SSP)
Slip next two stitches, one at a time, as to knit from left needle to right needle. Slip these stitches back onto left needle keeping them twisted.

Purl these two stitches together through back loops.

KITCHENER STITCH

This method of weaving with two needles is used for the toes of socks and flat seams. To weave the edges together and form an unbroken line of stockinette stitch, divide all stitches evenly onto two knitting needles—one behind the other. Thread yarn into tapestry needle. Hold needles with wrong sides together and work from right to left as follows:

Step 1: Insert tapestry needle into first stitch on front needle as to purl. Draw yarn through stitch, leaving stitch on knitting needle.

Step 2: Insert tapestry needle into the first stitch on the back needle as to purl. Draw yarn through stitch and slip stitch off knitting needle.

Step 3: Insert tapestry needle into the next stitch on same (back) needle as to knit, leaving stitch on knitting needle.

Step 4: Insert tapestry needle into the first stitch on the front needle as to knit. Draw yarn through stitch and slip stitch off knitting needle.

Step 5: Insert tapestry needle into the next stitch on same (front) needle as to purl. Draw yarn through stitch, leaving stitch on knitting needle.

Repeat Steps 2 through 5 until one stitch is left on each needle. Then repeat Steps 2 and 4. Fasten off. Woven stitches should be the same size as adjacent knitted stitches.

Knit Abbreviations & Symbols

approx · · · approximately
beg · · · begin/beginning
CC · · · · contrasting color
ch · · · · · · chain stitch
cm · · · · · centimeter(s)
cn · · · · · cable needle
dec · · decrease/decreases/ decreasing
dpn(s) · · double-pointed needle(s)
g · · · · · · · gram(s)
inc · · increase/increases/ increasing
k · · · · · · · · · knit
k2tog · · · knit 2 stitches together
LH · · · · · left hand
lp(s) · · · · · · loop(s)
m · · · · · · · meter(s)

M1 · · · · make one stitch
MC · · · · · main color
mm · · · · millimeter(s)
oz · · · · · · ounce(s)
p · · · · · · · · purl
pat(s) · · · · pattern(s)
p2tog · · · purl 2 stitches together
psso · pass slipped stitch over
p2sso · · · · pass 2 slipped stitches over
rem · · · remain/remaining
rep · · · · · · repeat(s)
rev St st · · · · reverse stockinette stitch
RH · · · · · · right hand
rnd(s) · · · · · round(s)
RS · · · · · · · right side

skp · · slip, knit, pass stitch over—1 stitch decreased
sk2p · · · · · slip 1, knit 2 together, pass slip stitch over the knit 2 together—2 stitches have been decreased
sl · · · · · · · · · · slip
sl 1k · · · slip 1 knitwise
sl 1p · · · slip 1 purlwise
sl st · · · slip stitch(es)
ssk · · slip, slip, knit these 2 stitches together—a decrease
st(s) · · · · · · · stitch(es)
St st · · · stockinette stitch/ stocking stitch
tbl · · through back loop(s)
tog · · · · · · · together
WS · · · · · · wrong side
wyib · · ·with yarn in back

wyif · · · with yarn in front
yd(s) · · · · · · · yard(s)
yfwd · · · · yarn forward
yo · · · · · · yarn over

[] work instructions within brackets as many times as directed

( ) work instructions within parentheses in the place directed

** repeat instructions following the asterisks as directed

* repeat instructions following the single asterisk as directed

" inch(es)

Knitting Needle Conversion Chart

U.S.	1	2	3	4	5	6	7	8	9	10	10½	11	13	15	17	19	35	50
Continental-mm	2.25	2.75	3.25	3.5	3.75	4	4.5	5	5.5	6	6.5	8	9	10	12.75	15	19	25

Crochet Stitch Guide

INTERNATIONAL CONVERSION CHARTS

The patterns in this book are written using American crochet stitch terminology.

For our international customers, hook sizes, stitches and yarn definitions should be converted as follows:

US		UK
sl st (slip stitch)	=	sc (single crochet)
sc (single crochet)	=	dc (double crochet)
hdc (half double crochet)	=	htr (half treble crochet)
dc (double crochet)	=	tr (treble crochet)
tr (treble crochet)	=	dtr (double treble crochet)
dtr (double treble crochet)	=	ttr (triple treble crochet)
skip	=	miss

CROCHET STITCHES

CHAIN STITCH (CH)

Begin by making a slip knot on the hook. Bring the yarn over the hook from back to front and draw through the loop on the hook.

For each additional chain stitch, bring the yarn over the hook from back to front and draw through the loop on the hook.

SLIP STITCH (SL ST)

Insert hook under both loops of the stitch, bring yarn over the hook from back to front and draw it through the stitch and the loop on the hook.

SINGLE CROCHET (SC)

Insert the hook in the second chain through the center of the V. Bring the yarn over the hook from back to front.

Draw the yarn through the chain stitch and onto the hook.

Again bring yarn over the hook from back to front and draw it through both loops on hook.

For additional rows of single crochet, insert the hook under both loops of the previous stitch instead of through the center of the V as when working into the chain stitch.

REVERSE SINGLE CROCHET (REVERSE SC)

Working in opposite direction from single crochet, insert hook under both loops of the next stitch to the right.

Bring yarn over hook from back to front and draw through both loops on hook.

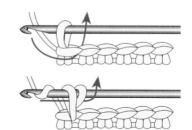

HALF-DOUBLE CROCHET (HDC)

Bring yarn over hook from back to front, insert hook in indicated chain stitch.

Draw yarn through the chain stitch and onto the hook.

Bring yarn over the hook from back to front and draw it through all three loops on the hook in one motion.

DOUBLE CROCHET (DC)

Yo, insert hook in st, yo, pull through st, (yo, pull through 2 lps) 2 times.

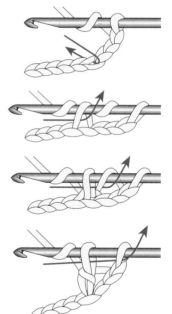

TREBLE CROCHET (TR)

Yo 2 times, insert hook in st, yo, pull through st, (yo, pull through 2 lps) 3 times.

DOUBLE TREBLE CROCHET—DTR

Yo 3 times, insert hook in st, yo, pull through st, [yo, pull through 2 lps], 4 times.

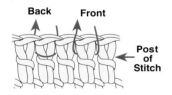

FRONT POST STITCH— FP: BACK POST STITCH—BP:

When working post st, insert hook from right to left around post st on previous row.

FRONT LOOP—FRONT LP BACK LOOP— BACK LP

CHANGE COLORS:

Drop first color; with 2nd color, pull through last 2 lps of st.

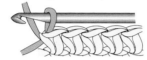

SINGLE CROCHET DECREASE (SC DEC):

(Insert hook, yo, draw lp through) in each of the sts indicated, yo, draw through all lps on hook.

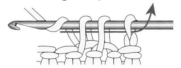

HALF DOUBLE CROCHET DECREASE (HDC DEC):

(Yo, insert hook, yo, draw lp through) in each of the sts indicated, yo, draw through all lps on hook.

DOUBLE CROCHET DECREASE (DC DEC):

(Yo, insert hook, yo, draw loop through, draw through 2 lps on hook) in each of the sts indicated, yo, draw through all lps on hook.

Crochet Hooks Conversion Chart

U.S.	1/B	2/C	3/D	4/E	5/F	6/G	8/H	9/I	10/J	10½/K	N
Continental-mm	2.25	2.75	3.25	3.5	3.75	4.25	5	5.5	6	6.5	9.0

Felting Instructions

Place items to be felted in the washing machine along with one tablespoon of dish soap and a pair of jeans or other laundry. (Remember, do not wash items you wish to felt with other clothing that releases its own fibers, or you will have these fibers in your project.) Set washing machine on smallest load using hot water. Start the machine and check the progress after ten minutes. Check progress more frequently after piece starts to felt. Reset the machine, if needed, to continue the agitation cycle. Do not allow machine to drain and spin until the piece is the desired size; creases can form in the fabric during the rapid spin cyle. As the piece becomes more felted, you may need to pull it into shape. When the piece has felted to the desired size, rinse it gently by hand in warm water. Do not use a cold water rinse as it will shock the fibers and cause them to felt even more. Remove the excess water either by rolling in a towel and squeezing, or in the spin cycle of your washing machine.

Block the piece into shape, and let air dry. Do not dry in clothes dryer. Felted items are very strong, so don't be afraid to push and pull it into the desired shape. It may take several hours or several days for the pieces to dry completely.

After the piece is completely dry, excess fuzziness can be trimmed with scissors if a smoother surface is desired. Or the piece can be brushed for a fuzzier appearance.

General Information

Standard Yarn Weight System

Categories of yarn, gauge ranges, and recommended needle sizes

Yarn Weight Symbol & Category Names	**1** SUPER FINE	**2** FINE	**3** LIGHT	**4** MEDIUM	**5** BULKY	**6** SUPER BULKY
Type of Yarns in Category	Sock, Fingering, Baby	Sport, Baby	DK, Light Worsted	Worsted, Afghan, Aran	Chunky, Craft, Rug	Super Chunky, Roving
Knit Gauge Range* in Stockinette Stitch to 4 inches	27–32 sts	23–26 sts	21–24 sts	16–20 sts	12–15 sts	6–11 sts
Recommended Needle in Metric Size Range	2.25–3.25mm	3.25–3.75mm	3.75–4.5mm	4.5–5.5mm	5.5–8mm	8mm and larger
Recommended Needle U.S. Size Range	1 to 3	3 to 5	5 to 7	7 to 9	9 to 11	11 and larger

* GUIDELINES ONLY: The above reflect the most commonly used gauges and needle sizes for specific yarn categories.

Inches Into Millimeters & Centimeters

All measurements are rounded off slightly.

inches	mm	cm	inches	cm	inches	cm	inches	cm	inches	cm
⅛	3	0.3	3	7.5	13	33.0	26	66.0	39	99.0
¼	6	0.6	3½	9.0	14	35.5	27	68.5	40	101.5
⅜	10	1.0	4	10.0	15	38.0	28	71.0	41	104.0
½	13	1.3	4½	11.5	16	40.5	29	73.5	42	106.5
⅝	15	1.5	5	12.5	17	43.0	30	76.0	43	109.0
¾	20	2.0	5½	14	18	46.0	31	79.0	44	112.0
⅞	22	2.2	6	15.0	19	48.5	32	81.5	45	114.5
1	25	2.5	7	18.0	20	51.0	33	84.0	46	117.0
1¼	32	3.8	8	20.5	21	53.5	34	86.5	47	119.5
1½	38	3.8	9	23.0	22	56.0	35	89.0	48	122.0
1¾	45	4.5	10	25.5	23	58.5	36	91.5	49	124.5
2	50	5.0	11	28.0	24	61.0	37	94.0	50	127.0
2½	65	6.5	12	30.5	25	63.5	38	96.5		

Skill Levels

BEGINNER
Beginner projects using basic stitches. Minimal shaping.

EASY
Easy projects using basic stitches, repetitive stitch patterns, simple color changes and simple shaping and finishing.

INTERMEDIATE
Intermediate projects with a variety of stitches, mid-level shaping and finishing.

EXPERIENCED
Experienced projects using advanced techniques and stitches, detailed shaping and refined finishing.

Buyer's Guide

BROWN SHEEP CO. INC.
100662 County Road 16
Mitchell, Nebraska 69357
(800) 826-9136
www.brownsheep.com

BUTTONS ETC.
2 Heitz Place
Hicksville, NY 11801
(800) 237-0613
www.buttonsetc.com

CARON INTERNATIONAL
Customer Service
P.O. Box 222
Washington, NC 27889
www.caron.com

COATS & CLARK
(Red Heart, Moda Dea, TLC)
Consumer Services
P. O. Box 12229
Greenville, SC 29612-0229
(800) 648-1479
www.coatsandclark.com
www.modadea.com

KNIT ONE, CROCHET TOO INC.
91 Tandberg Trail, Unit 6
Windham, ME 04062
(207) 892-9625
www.knitonecrochettoo.com

LILY CHIN SIGNATURE COLLECTION
5333 Casgrain #1204
Montreal, QC
H2T 1X3 Canada
(877) 244-1204
www.lilychinsignaturecollection.com

LION BRAND YARN CO.
135 Kero Road
Carlstadt, NJ 07072
(800) 258-YARN (9276)
www.lionbrand.com

LOUET NORTH AMERICA
3425 Hands Road
Prescott, ON
K0E 1T0 Canada
(613) 925-4502
www.louet.com

N.Y. YARNS/TAHKI-STACY CHARLES INC.
70-30 80th St. Bldg. 36
Ridgewood, NY 11385
(718) 326-4433
www.nyyarns.com
www.tahkistacycharles.com

PLYMOUTH YARN CO. INC
500 Lafayette St.
Bristol, PA 19007
(215) 788-0459
www.plymouthyarn.com

S.R. KERTZER (Twilleys of Stamford)
6060 Burnside Court
Unit 2
Mississauga, ON
L5T 2T5 Canada
(800) 263-2354
www.kertzer.com

SOUTH WEST TRADING CO.
(866) 794-1818
www.soysilk.com

SPINRITE YARNS
(Bernat, Patons)
320 Livingstone Ave. S.
Listowel, ON
N4W 3H3 Canada
(888) 368-8401
www.bernat.com
www.patonsyarns.com

UNIVERSAL YARN INC.
284 Ann St., Concord, NC 28025
(877) UniYarn (864-9276)
www.universalyarn.com

Special Thanks

We would like to thank the talented designers whose work is featured in this collection.

Gayle Bunn
Classic Cables Vest, 131
Tempting Texture, 165
Twisted Cable Dog Coat, 86

Anita Closic
Tranquil Pillow Trio, 153

Nazanin S. Fard
Baby Basket Beanie & Blankie, 21
Simple Cables Set, 76

Julie Gaddy
Intriguing Shadows Place Mats, 61
Perfect Sash, 84
Tampa Vest, 96

Sara Louise Harper
Cool Felted Hangers, 58
Fun & Felted Bag, 64

Shari Haux
Chain Reaction, 135

Katharine Hunt
Sporty Tea Cozy, 48

Melissa Leapman
City Girl Cardigan, 118

Bobbie Matela
Alluring Shawl, 51

Debbie O'Neill
Cabled Wishes Pullover, 122
Traveler's Jacket, 106

Kathy Perry
On-the-Go Baby Set, 35
Play Misty, 114

Celeste Pinheiro
Holey Moley Scarf, 72
Memory Book Cover, 46
Zigzag Waves, 74

Cindy Polfer
My Little Monkey Romper & Blankie, 24

Susan Robicheau
Warm Their Toes, 79

Kathy Sasser
Chic & Cabled Top, 101

Sandy Scoville
Dashing Hues, 142
Woven Splendor, 148

E.J. Slayton
Dynamic Vest, 126
Playtime Baby Set, 39

Jodi Snyder
Captivating Bolero, 92

Scarlet Taylor
Garter Stripes Ensemble, 16
Peace of Mind Hoodie, 110

Kennita Tully
Diagonal Eyelets Baby Set, 12
Precious Bundle Set, 30
Vine Lace, 162

Christine L. Walter
Magical Leaves, 156
Not-So-Square Hat and Scarf Set, 67
Wanderlust Cap, 82
Winning Waves, 159

Kathy Wesley
Diamond Twist Afghan, 150
Handy Hostess Set, 54
Pleasure Colors, 140

Diane Zangl
Stadium Blanket, 145